Books by James Thomas Flexner

American Painting

FIRST FLOWERS OF OUR WILDERNESS

THE LIGHT OF DISTANT SKIES

THAT WILDER IMAGE

THE POCKET HISTORY OF AMERICAN PAINTING
(also published as *A Short History of American Painting*)

History and Biography

DOCTORS ON HORSEBACK
Pioneers of American Medicine

STEAMBOATS COME TRUE
(also published as *Inventors in Action*)

THE TRAITOR AND THE SPY
(also published as *The Benedict Arnold Case*)

MOHAWK BARONET
Sir William Johnson of New York

WILLIAM HENRY WELCH AND THE HEROIC AGE OF AMERICAN MEDICINE
(with Simon Flexner)

AMERICA'S OLD MASTERS

JOHN SINGLETON COPLEY

GILBERT STUART

THE WORLD OF WINSLOW HOMER
(with the editors of Time-Life Books)

GEORGE WASHINGTON
I. The Forge of Experience (1732–1775)
II. In the American Revolution (1775–1783)

The Double Adventure of
JOHN
SINGLETON
COPLEY

The Double Adventure of
JOHN
SINGLETON
COPLEY

First Major Painter of the New World

by
JAMES THOMAS FLEXNER

Boston   LITTLE, BROWN AND COMPANY   *Toronto*

This book is a reworking of material previously published in the author's books *America's Old Masters* and *John Singleton Copley.*

Published simultaneously in Canada
by Little, Brown & Company (Canada) Limited

PRINTED IN THE UNITED STATES OF AMERICA

CONTENTS

LIST OF ILLUSTRATIONS

The Double Adventure of
JOHN
SINGLETON
COPLEY

PROLOGUE

A STRANGE PICTURE

THE PICTURE STOOD against the wall of Sir Joshua Reynolds's studio, striking a strange note in that center of elegance. The great English painter scowled at it in amazement, for as he later explained, he had never seen a canvas that gave him quite the same feeling. There was a stiffness about this portrait of a young boy, a dryness of outline and a coldness of color, that seemed to stem from the imitators of Godfrey Kneller, the school of painting that Sir Joshua had himself overthrown. But the practitioners of that school never painted so realistically, with such powerful sincerity. And what was one to think of the strange animal that was represented standing on the table over which the boy leaned? It was eating a nut. The queer, tiny thing nibbled away quite as naturally as if there really were miniature squirrels in the world that had white membranes running from their bodies to their legs like the membranes of a bat. Indeed, the animal was so convincingly drawn one had to believe it really existed.

Sir Joshua turned to Lord Buchan, who had brought the picture into his studio, and asked the painter's name. Shrugging, the connoisseur replied that he

Bruce was to write home to Copley that Reynolds had said: "Considering the disadvantages you had labored under, it is a very wonderful performance. . . . He did not know one painter at home, who had all the advantages that Europe could give them, that could equal it, and that if you are capable of producing such a piece by the mere efforts of your own genius, with the advantages of example and instruction which you could have in Europe, you would be a valuable acquisition to the art and one of the first painters in the world." In fact, Reynolds was so excited that he forgot to write down the name of the painter. Thus it came about that the first picture of John Singleton Copley to be publicly exhibited anywhere in the world was mislabeled; the artist's name was given as "William Copley."

The romantic story of the masterpiece that had emerged unheralded from the wilderness soon spread through the compact art world of London. Connoisseurs flocked to see the picture of a provincial child leaning intently over a table where stood a strange animal. Soon the name of Copley was on every cultivated tongue. On the strength of this one picture the unknown and misnamed painter was given the highest honor the English art world could offer: he was elected a member of the Society of Artists. People wondered how such a genius could have sprung up under the shadow of America's primeval trees.

PROLOGUE

A STRANGE PICTURE

THE PICTURE STOOD against the wall of Sir Joshua Reynolds's studio, striking a strange note in that center of elegance. The great English painter scowled at it in amazement, for as he later explained, he had never seen a canvas that gave him quite the same feeling. There was a stiffness about this portrait of a young boy, a dryness of outline and a coldness of color, that seemed to stem from the imitators of Godfrey Kneller, the school of painting that Sir Joshua had himself overthrown. But the practitioners of that school never painted so realistically, with such powerful sincerity. And what was one to think of the strange animal that was represented standing on the table over which the boy leaned? It was eating a nut. The queer, tiny thing nibbled away quite as naturally as if there really were miniature squirrels in the world that had white membranes running from their bodies to their legs like the membranes of a bat. Indeed, the animal was so convincingly drawn one had to believe it really existed.

Sir Joshua turned to Lord Buchan, who had brought the picture into his studio, and asked the painter's name. Shrugging, the connoisseur replied that he could not remember; it was a name he had never heard before. The canvas had been left with him by an American sea captain he had met somewhere, so he assumed it was by an American. Indeed, he was sure of only one thing: the painter, whoever he was, wished to have the picture exhibited at the Society of Artists.

America was then still a colonial possession of Great Britain. Sir Joshua could hardly believe that so fine a picture could have been done by an unknown artist hidden away in that distant land. Eager to unravel the mystery, he summoned Benjamin West, an American-born painter who enjoyed great celebrity in London.

West took one look at the squirrel that had so confused Reynolds, laughed, and said he knew that type of animal well; flying squirrels had been part of his boyhood in Pennsylvania. Then he turned the picture on its back and stared at the frame on which the canvas was stretched. "That's American pine wood," he said. The picture was certainly by an American, but by what American? None of the Colonials in England painted in that style or so well. Ecstatically West praised the "delicious color worthy of Titian," and although Sir Joshua, who thought the coloring cold, winced at this, he agreed that the picture was excellent, more than good enough to exhibit at the Society of Artists. However, there was a rule against showing anonymous pictures; the name of the painter must be discovered and that at once.

West rushed out and questioned Joseph Wright, a young arrival from America who had, in West's words, "just made his appearance in the art in a surprising degree of merit." But Wright denied that he had painted the picture. From then on West and Reynolds scratched their heads in vain; they could think of nobody. Finally Reynolds was forced to send the canvas, although its painter was still unidentified, to the exhibition with his own pictures. He argued that the portrait was so outstanding it should be hung despite the rule against anonymous pictures, and the conservative academicians, after poring one by one over the strange canvas, agreed that an exception would have to be made for so remarkable a work of art.

However, before the exhibition opened, Lord Buchan hurried to Sir Joshua's studio, followed by a large seafaring American. Captain Bruce seemed out of place in the elegant chamber where hung many portraits of stylish ladies, but it was he who had brought the painting to Lord Buchan. It was done, he said, by a young Bostonian named Copley, John Singleton Copley. Sir Joshua looked at Bruce with increasing amazement as the sea captain told him that Copley, although twenty-eight years old, had never been out of the provincial city of Boston, and had never in his life seen a picture worthy to be called a painting.

Bruce was to write home to Copley that Reynolds had said: "Considering the disadvantages you had labored under, it is a very wonderful performance. . . . He did not know one painter at home, who had all the advantages that Europe could give them, that could equal it, and that if you are capable of producing such a piece by the mere efforts of your own genius, with the advantages of example and instruction which you could have in Europe, you would be a valuable acquisition to the art and one of the first painters in the world." In fact, Reynolds was so excited that he forgot to write down the name of the painter. Thus it came about that the first picture of John Singleton Copley to be publicly exhibited anywhere in the world was mislabeled; the artist's name was given as "William Copley."

The romantic story of the masterpiece that had emerged unheralded from the wilderness soon spread through the compact art world of London. Connoisseurs flocked to see the picture of a provincial child leaning intently over a table where stood a strange animal. Soon the name of Copley was on every cultivated tongue. On the strength of this one picture the unknown and misnamed painter was given the highest honor the English art world could offer: he was elected a member of the Society of Artists. People wondered how such a genius could have sprung up under the shadow of America's primeval trees.

TERROR ON LONG WHARF

THE TINY HOUSE in which John Singleton Copley had spent his childhood had flowing beneath it the water of Boston Bay. Since the harbor, much of which is now filled in with land, was then very shallow, the end of Boston's main street had been extended some two thousand feet out into the bay to form what was known as Long Wharf. The pier was so broad that houses were built along one side. It was in one of these that young Copley lived.

No one knows whether or not Copley was born on the wharf or even in Boston. No record of his birth has ever been found. It is clear, however, that both his parents were Irish. His mother, Mary Singleton, had grown up in County Clare. His father, Richard Copley, was probably the son of an alderman and sheriff in Limerick. Family tradition, which may or may not be accurate, states that the couple was married in 1735, and that they came to Boston the next year. If this tradition is correct, Copley was born in New England. Actual records reveal that the family was probably in Boston when he was one year old and was surely there when he was three.

As far as is known, the future painter was an only child. Certainly if he had any brothers or sisters they did not survive infancy. John celebrated his birthday on July 3. We cannot be altogether certain how old he was when each year that day rolled round. He may have been born in 1737, or perhaps in 1738. Since the evidence leans toward 1738, that is the date you will find in most encyclopedias and which will be accepted in this volume.

By the time the Copley family appeared in recorded American history — when John was three — they were selling tobacco in Boston, probably from their shop on Long Wharf. As is so often the case with simple people whose letters no one considers worth keeping, the first mention of them is in those records of court proceedings which are kept not for private but governmental reasons. During 1741, "Richard Copley, tobacconist of Boston," sued a sailor named George Hamilton for the considerable sum of two hundred pounds, representing the capital and interest on one hundred and eighty pounds he had lent Hamilton in 1739. Since Hamilton is described as also of Boston, the chances are that the original transaction was carried on in that city, which increases the probability that the Copleys were there when John was born, or at least a year thereafter.

The next information we have concerning the painter's father is that he was dead. On May 6, 1748, when
John was nine, his mother was granted administration
of the deceased father's estate. This did not mean that
John's father had just died. He may have died several
years before without the mother bothering to clear
up his affairs. She was doing so now in preparation
for bringing into the family a new man who would
be John's stepfather.

As part of the legal proceedings, a listing was made
of the dead father's possessions, with values given for
everything. This "inventory" reveals how few and
cheaply furnished were the rooms in which the future
painter spent most of his childhood. "The Green
Chamber" seems to have been the store from which
the Copleys sold tobacco. It contained, so the list tells
us, "one suit of green curtains," two chests, and one
quilt: they were worth only six pounds, ten shillings.
In the kitchen, where the cooking was done in the fire-
place, the cooking equipment considered of enough
value to list consisted only of a spit for turning meat,
two saucepans, and a ladle for skimming off the grease.
There were in addition two irons. As table service,
the Copleys had two brass and two iron candlesticks,
seven dishes and seven plates made of pewter. Since
no knives or forks or spoons were mentioned, the Copleys' eating utensils must have been thought almost

worthless. Perhaps they were whittled from wood.

There was one bedroom, and it doubled as a sitting room. Here was the family pride. Valued at forty-two pounds, ten shillings, this object was considered worth almost half the entire value of all the Copley furnishings. It was one of those tall four-poster beds which, when the curtains that stretched between high posts were drawn, served as a room within the room. Since no other bed appeared in the list, John probably slept in this one with his mother. Where he had slept when his father was alive we do not know: perhaps in a cot that was not worth listing or was now sold, perhaps on the floor in a blanket. The family owned two blankets.

The other valuable piece of furniture — a fragile object which the Copleys may well have brought with loving care across the ocean — was a "looking glass" worth all of seven pounds. "An old desk" and "six old chairs" added up to nine pounds. There were also three tablecloths and three towels.

Now come the fascinating aspects of the Copleys' possessions. Humbly situated as they were, they owned what the listing described as "twelve bound books, etc." This was for those days a considerable library. More amazing still: the restricted walls were decorated with "six prints and pictures." By distinguishing "prints" from "pictures" the maker of the list implied that the "pictures" were paintings. How at that time, when paintings were not common in New England, did two or more find their way into the simple tobacconist's shop where lived a boy who was to become a great painter?

As he grew up, first with both his parents and then with only his mother in the little house on Long Wharf, Copley saw from the back windows water lapping the foundation. From the front windows he had a view that would make any boy's heart swell with the romance of travel and far places. Separated from his house by only a fifteen-foot walk lay moored the square-rigged ships that brought Boston its prosperity; sometimes twenty or more were tied to the long quay. The day and the night as well were loud with the creaking of blocks, as square sails blossomed from tall masts.

Daily the future painter watched ships emerge tiny from between the outlying islands and grow ever larger until they lay tied up at rest by his front door. He watched the sailors stand dizzily in line high up in the rigging as they lashed down the furled sails. Then his mother's tobacco shop would be full of the sound of voices. Standing behind one of the chests, answering quickly demands for tobacco "cut, pigtail, or spun," the boy served mariners who had returned from the seven seas. These gaudy men with gold rings in their ears had been to Africa, where they had exchanged sperm candles and rum for slaves; they had then carried their human merchandise to the West Indies, where men were exchanged for molasses. And already there was a rumbling in the street as the barrels of molasses were rolled toward distilleries where they would be changed into more rum with which to obtain a new harvest of black slaves.

Sometimes, perhaps, the weatherbeaten sailors brought queer African idols into Mrs. Copley's tobacco shop, and the youngster stared in amazement at the brown grotesques that would in another hundred and fifty years inspire a school of painters as different from the work he was to do as it was possible to be. How stories must have leapt from mouth to mouth while the blue tobacco smoke drifted toward the ceiling. The sailors described silent bays on the fringes of jungles, where chiefs moved under canopies accompanied everywhere by a whisper of drums. Then the talk would make a sudden change to the Spanish mansions of the West Indies, white in a glaring sun, where gaily dressed young aristocrats scraped and bowed, while from behind barred windows hidden ladies played tinkling castanets — castanets that were drowned out by the tom-tom beat of slaves returning at evening from the fields. And there were the months of sailing to describe: seas calm or riotous; strange, half-human albatrosses that followed their ships; and sometimes blue lights gleaming from each of the swaying masts, the corposants that boded — who knows? — disaster or prosperity, and made even blaspheming boatswains pray.

Every day brought new excitements as the endless war in Europe unrolled. Pirate ships set out from Long Wharf with the blessings of the Commonwealth, half-hidden guns looming black behind their ports. The sailors who crowded into Mrs. Copley's shop for a last hunk of tobacco before the adventure began had cutlasses in their belts, and their voices were thin with anticipation. Watching pirate sails vanish down the horizon, an imaginative lad could coin endless visions of blood and glory. Then months later there would be a running of feet on Long Wharf and a staring from the tip as the privateer came home towing a prize. In 1748, when Copley was ten, the frigate *Bethel* out of Boston, armed with only fourteen guns and carrying only thirty-eight men, brought following docilely in her wake a great Spanish treasure ship of twenty-four guns. More than a hundred prisoners lay bound beneath her decks. The breathless rumor went around that in the Spaniard's hold were a hundred thousand pounds in ducats and doubloons.

We might expect any boy brought up in such an atmosphere to run off to sea at an early age, shipping as a cabin boy and returning at last equipped with strange oaths and cutlass wounds. Or, if he became a painter, we should expect his canvases to be enlivened with the dash of warlike adventure: battles, generals and privateers would be glorified. But we may search Copley's work in vain for such pictures as these; rarely has a great artist been so unreceptive to the possibilities of romance. Neither interested nor impressed by men of physical action, Copley idealized sensitive intellectual faces, portraying them so lovingly that they formed the subject matter of his finest portraits. And when, in the manner of his time, he did turn to scenes of war, his canvases revealed no taste for bloodshed. In the best of his battle pictures, *The Death of Major Pierson,* the eye is caught and held by a weeping group in the foreground; the wife and child of the dying hero wail, louder than the guns and the shouts of victory, their anguish at man's inhumanity to man.

Copley's few paintings of the sea are tinged with horror. In his *The Repulse of the Floating Batteries at Gibraltar,* he shows the ocean full of the writhing forms of dying men; half-naked, torn bodies struggle in every contortion of pain with the enveloping flood. Only one other of his important canvases, *Brook Watson and the Shark,* deals primarily with the ocean, and that is a brilliantly painted representation of nightmare. In the foreground, a naked and defenseless swimmer sprawls in a contortion of anguish; he is being attacked by a shark. Behind him several men in a small boat huddle together in helpless terror, or vainly gesture to give assistance when assistance is past hope. And the water in which the victim flounders is a sickly yellow-green, a stringy and repulsive element in which naked men are attacked by monsters.

Whenever Copley refers to ships or the sea in the many letters that have come down to us, he does so with displeasure. If he had to travel from Boston to New York and Philadelphia, he traveled by land, although the roads were then so bad that water offered a much quicker and more comfortable route. As we shall see, Copley hesitated for years before he made the trip across the ocean so necessary to a Colonial painter, and he could never force himself to return.

Eighteenth-century seafaring was not altogether romantic; there was another side that might impress a lad more sensitive than adventuresome. Watching from his mother's window, Copley saw rebellious sailors being hung by their hands from the masts for punishment. He heard the cut of whips on naked backs. Battered, wincing derelicts limped into Mrs. Copley's shop — seamen who had been drafted in the inhuman manner of those days — knocked down on English streets and carried off without a word to their families. Their hands trembled when they picked up the tobacco the boy dealt out to them. In 1747, Commodore Charles Knowles tried this British custom in Boston. Annoyed by desertions, he landed a gang of armed sailors that kidnapped apprentices as they strolled down Long Wharf. Then the Boston populace rose and rioted for three long days, while the royal governor fled to Castle William and the naval commander threatened to bombard the town. With anxious eyes, the nine-year-old Copley watched sails rise on the British frigate as it maneuvered into position. But the commodore did not shoot and in the end was forced to release the men he had stolen.

The slave trade, too, showed its horrors. The West Indian planters, most of whose black imports died anyway during the first five years on the steaming and unhealthy plantations, would buy only prime human stock. Negroes who had sickened but not died during the long voyage from Africa, children born on the voyage or accepted in the jungle as a compromise to close a deal—these found no buyers. The traders were forced to ship such defective merchandise on to Boston and sell it for what it would bring as domestic servants. How often Copley must have seen black children of his own age unloaded with the barrels of molasses, driven in terrified groups down Long Wharf to the markets to be sold. How often he must have seen pitiful, staggering Negroes, once the pride of Africa, hustled off ships which no longer had room for them and allowed to die, being too weak to have any further value.

Flanking Mrs. Copley's shop on Long Wharf were grog shops which made the night hideous with the sound of drunken singing and fights. We need not be surprised that Copley reacted violently against his childhood environment. Persuaded later by his own children to talk of those unhappy days, he told them that he had escaped from the brutal reality into the recesses of his own mind; he became a quiet and studious lad. When the tough waterfront boys saw his pale face at the window and dared him to come out, hooting him as a sissy, he turned away from the window and occupied himself drawing pictures on the walls of the room. Family tradition tells us that at seven or eight he sketched in charcoal a group of martial figures engaged in some unnamed adventure. The Bible also was a source of inspiration to the well-brought-up lad, who showed his literal-mindedness by painting the sea Moses crossed a glowing red. Or did he think of all oceans as tinged with blood?

ENTER A STEPFATHER

ON MAY 22, 1748, just before John Copley's tenth birthday, he watched his mother walk to the altar and accept a new husband. The bridegroom was called Peter Pelham. He was fifty-three, undoubtedly much older than John's mother. He had been married twice before and had several grown sons.

Whatever the boy's emotions were at his mother's marriage to this elderly semi-stranger, there was one obvious, immediate advantage to come. John made his escape from the waterfront and its bullies. An advertisement soon appeared in the *Boston News Letter:* "Mrs. Mary Pelham (formerly the Widow Copley on Long Wharf, tobacconist)" had moved to "Lindel's Row, against the Quaker Meeting House, where she continues to sell the best Virginia tobacco, cut, pigtail and spun, by wholesale or retail, at the cheapest rates."

Although he did not make enough money to enable the former Widow Copley to give up her tobacco business, Peter Pelham was endlessly busy contributing to what today's newspapers would call "the cultural

life of Boston." John, who became well-educated as
the letters of his later years reveal, probably attended
his stepfather's "writing and arithmetic school" which,
so another advertisement stated, would be open during the winter season "from candle-light 'till nine in
the evening as usual, for the benefit of those employed
in business all day."

But Copley's new stepfather was no dry-as-dust
schoolteacher. Peter Pelham may indeed have dozed
sometimes as his students droned away at writing and
arithmetic. The elderly Englishman's heart was in ac-
complishments more elegant than the ordinary routine
of education. He had at one time advertised that he
would teach "young gentlemen and ladies" of Boston
needlework, painting, and dancing. It was the dancing
that had got him into trouble. The balls over which
he presided were immediately criticized by the New
England Puritans. "What could give encouragement
to so licentious and expensive a diversion in a town famous for its decency and good order?" an indignant
citizen asked in the Boston *Gazette*. "When we look
back upon the transactions of our forefathers and read
the wonderful story of their godly zeal, their pious resolution, and their public virtues, how should we blush
and lament our present corruption of manners and
decay of religious and civil discipline. . . . In vain
will our ministers preach charity, moderation, and hu-

mility to an audience whose thoughts are engaged in scenes of splendour and magnificence, and whose time and money are consumed in dress and dancing."

Prudery hampered the artistic-minded of Boston at every turn. During Copley's thirteenth year, the town had the excitement of its first theatrical performance. When two English actors announced that they would present *An Orphan, or Unhappy Marriage* at the British Coffee House and persuaded some rash Bostonians to take the minor roles, the citizens were so shocked at the idea of a play that everyone wanted to see it. A huge crowd gathered outside the coffee house, on King Street near Copley's home. Finding that there would not be room inside for all, they rioted. Then with the entire approval of the mob that had been so eager to get in the government passed an "Act to Prevent Stage Plays and Other Theatrical Entertainments," on the grounds that they "occasioned unnecessary expenses, discouraged industry," and encouraged "immorality, impiety, and contempt for religion." This law was passed again as late as 1784.

Yet Bostonians continued to give private balls. Mr. Pelham undoubtedly still taught dancing — although in a less conspicuous way — after he had become John's stepfather. More important, however, for the boy's future, was Mr. Pelham's basic profession. He was an artist-craftsman who had turned to teaching because there was not enough demand in Boston for the pictures he created.

Born in England, probably during 1695, Peter Pelham had been apprenticed at the age of eighteen to an engraver named John Simon. The trade he learned was in great demand in those days before the invention of photography and of mechanical methods for transferring a photograph onto a printer's plate. During Pelham's and Copley's lifetimes, a printed picture had to be made from start to finish by hand.

First, there being no lens and film to undertake the task, an artist had to create the image to be reproduced. For a humble illustration, the model to be copied might be no more than a line drawing. But Pelham was not dedicated to such humbler aspects of the engraver's craft. He learned to reproduce on metal, in a manner that would transfer to paper, small versions of those formal and complicated pictures: portraits painted in oil. He further learned enough about oil painting to be able himself to create at life-size (so that it could be hung on the wall as an independent work of art) the portrait which he would then reduce onto an engraver's plate. However, like most engravers, he preferred to reproduce, as more salable, the work of a painter more expert and celebrated than he.

Pelham's first step in preparing an engraving of an

oil painting was to make a copy the size of his printing plate in which the effect of color was indicated,
as far as possibility and his skill permitted, in shades
of black and white. This image was then transferred
to a flat piece of metal. Next, by scraping bits of the
metal away with various tools or eating them away
with acid, Pelham arranged on the plate what were
in effect tiny wells that would hold the ink. Before
printing, he spread ink over the entire plate and then
wiped away all that the wells did not retain. Finally,
he squeezed plate and paper together at exactly the
right pressure in a hand-operated press.

Mr. Pelham published some twenty-five engravings
in London between 1720 and 1726. This output indicated that he was achieving success. However he
seems to have got into some kind of trouble — exactly
what the records do not reveal — which made him de-
part from England. He sailed to America in 1727,
some ten years before Copley was born.

To practice his profession in the New World,
Peter Pelham needed to find — or, if necessary make
— oil portraits of persons so famous that many people
would be interested in buying the printed reproductions he sold. In small, compact, thickly populated,
aristocratic England this was a minor problem, but before the Revolution few Americans stood out. What
reputations were achieved usually did not travel the

wilderness miles from one city to another. Further-
more, Massachusetts suffered from a dearth of portrait
painters whose canvases Pelham could copy. He did
the best he could, sometimes himself painting (not
too skillfully) the oil originals. Yet the engravings he
was able to publish were few indeed.

When he married the Widow Copley, Pelham was
undoubtedly a disappointed man. Whatever had been
the ambitions of his youth, they certainly had not
been achieved. He could not know when he added a
ten-year-old stepson to his family that in John Copley's small body glowed the opportunity which life
had so far denied him, the glorious opportunity to
serve great art. The most important act of Pelham's
life was opening to the boy the door of his workroom.

What a marvelous refuge for the lad who had already found in making pictures an escape from the
wounds inflicted by the world! Here was the scarred
table on which Pelham made his prints; here were all
the sharp and intricate tools of the engraver's craft.
The stepfather, we know, taught the boy at least the
rudiments of engraving. Here too, although perhaps
dusty from lack of use, were materials and paints Pelham employed for his occasional oil paintings. Surely
he sometimes allowed the boy to dabble in bright colors, to spread paint with soft, imported brushes. Or,
first making certain that John's hands were clean, he

might bring down from a shelf the prints after English paintings that he sold, whenever he could, to what Colonial collectors there were. Copley fingered in excitement these reproductions of famous and far-away art, wondering whether an American could ever do as well.

Chance had thrown the boy Copley into one of the few households in all the Colonies where art was the predominant interest.

THE PAST OF AMERICAN PAINTING

PAINTING had had a long history in British America
—the earliest surviving canvases date from the 1660's
—but it had usually been created on what we would
today consider not a fine arts but an artisan level.
The workmen came from the humbler classes, for gentlemen, although willing to dabble a little in an
amateurish way, regarded a serious interest in art as beneath their social station. After Governor Gooch of
Virginia had been induced to lend his coach to an artist, he complained that "it looks a little odd for a governor to show so much favor to a painter."

A typical early American painter was at an early
age apprenticed to a trade: clockmaking, or saddling,
or if he were very lucky, house and sign painting.
After becoming twenty-one and setting out for himself, he followed the natural pattern of artisans in com-
munities so small and isolated that each contained
only a few workmen skilled with their hands and no
extensive market for any one kind of product. As his
neighbors expressed a need for various things, an artisan would add new occupations to his stock in trade,

becoming proficient in a half-dozen specialties. If people offered to pay him for painted pictures, and if he had an interest in design and could buy the necessary colors, he would go into that business too. If he were successful enough, art would grow to overshadow his other crafts.

On a sign-painting level there was a steady demand for every kind of picture: painted hats to identify haberdasheries, heroes on horseback to hang in front of taverns; murals that would decorate walls at less cost than imported wallpaper. But on the level of painting that could be regarded as a fine art, only portraiture was in considerable demand. A desire to put on canvas such wild scenery as the new continent offered did not emerge until the nineteenth century, when the romantic movement brought with it an admiration for untamed nature. Decorative paintings of a quality suited to gentlemen's houses were commonly imported with other luxuries from abroad. Portraits might also have been imported if written descriptions of what a person looked like could have enabled an English painter to produce a recognizable likeness. This was tried but it never worked out satisfactorily. Likenesses *did* have to be painted in the presence of the sitter. And such pictures eventually came to be regarded by prosperous Americans as a kind of necessity.

Colonial America, in which men created farms and

cities where only wilderness had previously been, had always encouraged self-reliance and individual pride. What successful citizen did not consider himself worthy of having his portrait painted? Even the Puritans, who were so strongly opposed to pictures in churches that religious paintings were rarely attempted in Colonial times, gloried in their own importance as creators of the New Jerusalem. And less pious Americans, who had taken advantage of the business opportunities offered by the New World to raise themselves by their own bootstraps, were fascinated by the romance of their careers. Everyone felt that dynasties were springing from them, and they could not bear the thought that their descendants would not see their features. Another source of business for portrait painters was the geographic separation of families: settlers sent their likenesses back home to Europe across the water.

Portraits were turned out in thousands by hundreds of painters. According to the traditional standards of European art, the pictures were without exception crude. No record demonstrates that before Copley's generation any American-born painter visited the galleries of the Old World. No record demonstrates that any truly beautiful pictures crossed the ocean from Europe to serve as an inspiration and academy for American painters. Artists who wanted to practice

European styles had to work them out from written descriptions in books or from the black and white engravings, all of them much smaller than the painted originals, that came across the water. Sources so inadequate were more likely to confuse than instruct. Usually the more an artist wished to paint in a sophisticated European manner, the less effective was his work. The early Colonial artists were at their strongest when they used their own eyes and made the wisest and most adventuresome use they could of the limited skills they really possessed.

When fate entered the shop of a naturally gifted Colonial artisan, and placed a paintbrush in the hand that had just put down a saw or a saddler's tool, she inspired an agile mind to struggle on its own with the eternal problems of art. Never having seen how Raphael had lighted a hand or how the London portrait master, Sir Peter Lely, had folded a drapery, the artist worked such matters out for himself. If he achieved a solution it was deeply felt, profoundly his own.

During the nineteenth century, it is true, Americans blushed with embarrassment at the roughness of our most original early portraits, and often commissioned restorers to repaint an ancestor into more acceptable shape. But today we recognize the great virtue of those pictures, which are called in the books American "Primitive" or "Folk" or "Naïve Art." Although simply conceived and flatly painted, the best of them have that freshness of unspoiled vision which is found in the work of gifted children, combined with the direction and power of maturity.

Occasionally, the early American painters were joined by artists from abroad. These artists were usually very simple craftsmen whose names were unknown to the great practitioners of the European courts; they brought with them provincial styles almost as crude as the work of their American contemporaries. The great exception to this rule was John Smibert, the artist who was to play so important a role in Copley's development.

A Scot by birth, Smibert began his career humbly enough as an apprentice to an Edinburgh house painter and plasterer. As soon as he was released from this bondage he journeyed to London, where he struggled to overcome his lack of social position and his lack of training, to become a portrait painter. Finally, fortune presented him with a three-year trip to Italy. Being able to boast of foreign study, he was on his return a successful portraitist; not one of the most fashionable and skillful, but still a well-trained man of reputation. The connoisseurs were amazed when he gave up his hard-earned position to join the radical philosopher Dean Berkeley, in a scheme to found in Bermuda a college for the education of the Indians. During 1728, ten years before Copley was born, Smibert accompanied Berkeley's party of idealists to Newport. There they waited for promised funds that never came.

After Bishop Berkeley's plan had finally collapsed, Smibert settled in Boston, where he made a rich marriage and established a virtual monopoly of the portrait business. A friend and business associate of Pelham, who made engravings after at least six of his portraits, he probably gave Copley some instruction. We know the boy saw hanging in Smibert's studio the copies the English painter had made of European masterpieces, including the one of Van Dyck's *Cardinal Bentivoglio* that was by itself to constitute the first American art school. Copley, Washington Allston, and John Trumbull, three of America's leading painters, all found in this one picture their first hints of a richer portrait style.

We can visualize Copley, not yet in his teens, bent with aching attention over the copies that brought him a pale reflection of great art. Twenty years later when he was himself a famous artist he was to see the originals and write home that Smibert's copies were inaccurate, miscolored, and badly drawn. But as a boy he was deeply impressed. There in the studio of a disgruntled English painter of medium ability the muses whispered in the ears of the Colonial genius who had never seen a well-painted picture.

However, Copley's period of instruction under Peter Pelham and John Smibert was short, for they both died in 1751. Pelham's estate was so small that his widow did not trouble to file an inventory; and there was another mouth in the family to feed, for Copley now had a half-brother, Henry Pelham. Again poverty faced the boy who had suffered the horrors of Long Wharf. By the time he was fifteen, he was trying to make money at the trade for which he was being trained. He set up as a painter and engraver.

FIRST STEPS OF A GENIUS

COPLEY'S FIRST ACT to earn something from art was to take an engraved plate his stepfather had made of the Rev. William Cooper, erase the head and that part of the inscription which gave the sitter's and the artist's names, add a different head and also a different inscription, which identified the print as a portrait of the Rev. William Welsteed, and claim the work as altogether his own. This plate printed and some copies (we hope) sold, Copley turned his back forever on engraving. He would not follow his stepfather's profession. Whatever the pitfalls, he would aim higher and become a painter.

In Europe, he would have had to serve a long apprenticeship, but taste in Boston was not demanding and the city suffered from a shortage of painters. By the time he was fifteen Copley was securing commissions.

Benjamin West, the American painter whose celebrity in London still lay years ahead of him, was exactly Copley's age. He was then making an equally successful start as a teen-age professional in his native

Pennsylvania. Such good fortune encouraged West to work with all the slapdash confidence usually associated with self-enchanted young prodigies. However, Copley's temperament was the opposite of West's. While West slashed away happily in his part of America, painting from his imagination castles and Romans in togas, as well as the faces he actually saw, Copley was bending in Boston over his canvases in an agony of indecision. Every feature he painted was questioned, rubbed out a dozen times, and then allowed to remain at last only because the picture had to be finished. If the boy whose childhood had been a round of terror possessed any self-confidence, it was the grim determination of the frightened who fight lest they perish.

The voluminous correspondence of Copley's later years makes clear that it was natural to his character to seek instruction wherever he could find it. He certainly consulted all the artists and studied all the paintings that came his way. During his childhood, there was the example of Pelham and Smibert, and also that of Robert Feke, the mariner from Oyster Bay who is generally conceded to have been the best American-born painter before Copley and West, and who practiced in Boston during 1748-1749. Although the boy was only eleven when Feke went away, he may easily have studied during his teens some of the admirable canvases that the gay and primitive master left behind him.

After Smibert, Pelham, and Feke had died or left, two greatly inferior artists, Joseph Badger and John Greenwood, practiced in Boston. They were the rivals, perhaps the inspirers, of Copley's first professional efforts, which were made when he was about fifteen. Badger, the son of a poor tailor, had been trained as a house painter and glazier; that he moved in very simple circles is shown by the fact that his wife was illiterate. He imitated Smibert and copied stock poses from English prints. Filling in the gaps from his own imagination, he painted canvases which, despite their muddy color and clumsy drawing, have a naïve sincerity that gives them a certain charm. They were considered such wonders of art that for ten years he was the most admired painter in New England.

Second to Badger was Greenwood, who had learned to paint as an apprentice to a maker of charts and coats of arms. His style was more nervous and sensitive, but he had the disadvantage of coming from a relatively sophisticated background; he recognized his lack of training and thus never attained the childlike self-sufficiency that makes some of Badger's canvases delightful worlds of their own.

As he veered toward one influence or another, the

canvases Copley painted when he was about fifteen reveal little of his own personality, and are indeed
contradictory. Very ambitious was his group portrait
of four Gore children. The young sitters have iden-
tical pretty faces which show no observation of nature;
the poses seem to have been variously inspired by various works of various of his Colonial predecessors. As
for the landscape in the background, it is a confec-
tioner's concoction (probably copied from a print),
complete with ornamental bridge and sailboat. Each
child's dress is painted a different color: one yellow,
one blue, one pink, one tobacco brown. The picture
shows that Copley had great potential gifts as a painter, but that for the moment he was applying it to nothing of his own.

The head Copley put into the Welsteed engraving
had been in Badger's style. The companion canvases
of a fashionable young couple, Mr. and Mrs. Joseph
Mann, render conventional compositions based on
English prints in a style that seems a mingling of Smibert and Feke, with just a touch of Greenwood.

Copley was floundering, like an inexperienced sail-
or who changes his course for every puff of breeze,
when suddenly a great wind arose. In 1755, there appeared in Boston a traveling artist, Joseph Blackburn,
who practiced a somewhat simplified variation of the
most fancy of all contemporary English portrait styles.

THE BROTHERS AND SISTERS OF CHRISTOPHER GORE
(The Gore Children)
Circa 1755. Oil on canvas. 40½ x 56¼.
Courtesy of the Henry Francis du Pont Winterthur Museum

Opposite in temperament to the sober and heavy Smibert, Blackburn exuded gay lightheartedness. He covered his ladies, as if they were Christmas trees, with looping festoons of pearls. He had a gift for graceful poses quite unlike the stiff mannerisms of the local artists, and he showed an almost feminine affection for laces and satins. His colors were sensitive and glowing. But the faces he painted were too generalized, each according to some conventional formula, to be powerful likenesses. As a whole, his pictures lacked strength.

Although Copley, who was doing portraits on his own, could never have been Blackburn's apprentice, he enthusiastically imitated the newcomer's virtues, not hesitating to borrow entire conceptions if they pleased him. When Blackburn painted a Colonial belle as a shepherdess with a crook in her hand and a lamb by her side, Copley did the same for one of his own sitters. By such means he quickly assimilated the grace of his elder's style, and then he was the better painter, for he was developing to a superlative degree that quality Blackburn lacked: the ability to depict character in faces. By the time he was nineteen, Copley's fame had traveled so far that he was invited to Nova Scotia. "There are several people who would be glad to employ you," wrote Thomas Ainslie of Halifax. "I believe so because I have heard it mentioned."

Copley, however, did not go, perhaps because the idea of travel terrified him.

The boy who had huddled behind locked doors on Long Wharf had become a self-contained young man who worked at his trade with passionate intensity and rarely went out in the world. The popular historical novelist who depicted him as turning up at a drunken brawl at Harvard and taking the blame when angry college authorities appeared could hardly have distorted his character further from what the evidence shows. By nature afraid of his fellow men, painfully conscious that he practiced a socially inferior profession, Copley carried sober respectability to the extreme. The worst that is recorded against him is that a selectman once caught him strolling on the Sabbath. Gravely he explained that he worked so hard during the week, he had to take exercise on Sunday for his health.

When Copley had with methodical industry learned all that he could from Blackburn, he was the best painter in the Colonies, but he was conscious that his work was still crude. There was that matter of eyes, for instance; no one in America could paint an eye that did not look like a slit cut into a mask. If only he could find good models to imitate! He was to tell his children that he had been entirely self-taught and had never seen a decent picture while a young man. He was to write Benjamin West: "In this country, as you rightly observe, there is no example of art except what is to [be] met with in a few prints indifferently executed, from which it is not possible to learn much. . . . I think myself particularly unlucky in living in a place into which there has not been one portrait brought that is worthy to be called a picture within my memory, which leaves me at a great loss to guess the style that you, Mr. Reynolds, and other artists practice."

Seeking, perhaps, for a quicker medium than oil paint in which to try experiments, Copley determined to draw portraits with crayons, producing what are known as pastels. He had in all probability seen only a few indifferent examples of this art, some by Blackburn, and certainly he was not sure what kind of crayons to use. The books he read told him that the best living pastelist was Jean Étienne Liotard, who lived in Geneva and was famous for sentimental pieces such as his *Chocolate Girl,* now in the Dresden Gallery. In 1762 he wrote to Liotard, asking him to send "one set of crayons of the very best kind, such as you can recommend [for] liveliness, colour, and justness of tints. . . . You may perhaps be surprised that so remote a corner of the globe as New England should have any demand for the necessary utensils for practicing the fine arts, but I assure you, sir, however feeble our efforts may be, it is not for want of inclination that they are not better, but the want of opportunity to improve ourselves. However, America, which has been the seat of war and desolation [Copley was referring to the French and Indian War], I would fain hope will one day become the school of fine arts, and Monsieur Liotard['s] drawings with justice be set as patterns for our imitation." It was a nice compliment, but Copley was too truthful to keep from adding: "Not that I have ever had the advantage of beholding any one of these rare pieces from your hand, but [have] formed a judgment on the true taste of several of my friends who has seen [th]em." There is no indication that Liotard ever answered this letter. However, Copley used what crayons he could get, teaching himself to become America's earliest important draftsman in pastel.

Working in crayons gave Copley a refreshing feeling of release, for as he employed this lighter and quicker medium he was able to forget temporarily the profound problems that made his oil paintings an agonizing battle to record the basic forms of nature, the basic traits of humanity. His pastels are decorative, brightly colored, and for him superficial. He depicted Thomas Hancock both in crayon and oil. When making the drawing Copley shaped the features smoothly and broadly, creating a likeness that would be recognized by a friend but would give a stranger little idea of character. The painted head contains many more details, many more shapes and planes, yet gives the viewer's eye a more satisfactory impression of roundness. We see before us a vainglorious, shrewd, and stubborn fat man, the very merchant who ran up a few pounds into a great fortune.

At the age of about twenty-two, Copley drew his own picture in pastels. The result is on the whole disappointing. The smooth, heavy face reflects only dimly the intense, humorless, passionate, and restrained personality of the artist. Copley preferred to concentrate on depicting the fine silk of his lounging robe and the elaborate stuff of his waistcoat. Yet the uncommunicativeness of this portrait can be blamed only in part on the pastel medium. Copley never dissected himself as he dissected others; the oil self-portrait he painted many years later in England is more revealing than the crayon drawing, it is true, but it is not a really profound likeness. How unintrospective Copley was is shown by his belief, expressed in a letter to West, that his pastels were among his best pictures, a belief inspired perhaps less by the drawings themselves than by the carefree pleasure he had in creating them.

In those days before the camera could supply small prints, there was a steady demand for portraits so tiny that they could be enclosed in gold cases which

SELF-PORTRAIT OF JOHN SINGLETON COPLEY
1769. Pastel. 23¾ x 17½.
Courtesy of the Henry Francis du Pont Winterthur Museum.

ladies wore as ornaments or men carried in their pock-
ets. Copley now undertook such pictures, sometimes
painting them in oil on tiny sheets of copper, more
commonly drawing them in watercolor on chips of
ivory. This second manner had a great advantage
which made it popular with artists and purchasers.
Since watercolor is transparent, the light that shines
on the picture passes through it and is then reflected
back by the shiny ivory, giving the image some of
the brightness that would be achieved were it actually
lighted from behind.

Meant to be personal keepsakes more intimate than
full-size portraits, such little likenesses needed no more
than to suggest the presence of a loved one. Copley
tended to indicate the general shape of a head, add
the most obvious features, and then consider the portrait complete. The figures crowd the frames in the
typical eighteenth-century manner, and the shoulders
drop in steep lines that have little relation to nature
but make a satisfactory design. Copley, who was a rug-
ged artist, seems not to have been really interested in
delicacy and a small scale, yet he was too able to do
anything badly. His little oils on copper are sometimes
surprisingly strong, and his miniatures on ivory, with
their harmonious details and their fresh color, rank
with the best created by his Colonial contemporaries.

However, before many years had passed Copley

abandoned miniature painting altogether as bringing too low a price. His increasing fame had brought him sitters of higher social position until now his studio was filled with the most prosperous citizens of Boston. The depression that had followed the French and Indian War was over and the bright sun of prosperity seemed to have shriveled up the popular party of men like Samuel Adams, who a few years before had almost started an insurrection in the name of a land bank and cheap money. There was nothing to indicate that in fifteen years the country would be torn by revolution. In refusing another invitation to Halifax, Copley wrote during 1765: "I have a large room full of pictures unfinished which would engage me these twelve months if I did not begin any others. . . . I assure you I have been as fully employed these several years past as I could expect or wish to be, as more would be a means to retard the design I have always had in view, that of improving in that charming art which is my delight, and gaining a reputation, rather than a fortune without that."

Copley, however, was not indifferent to the sums he earned, for he had known poverty too well in his youth not to recognize its power of bringing unhappiness. He felt that in the materialistic Colonies he could command respect only if he became rich. The low opinion in which Americans held art filled

him with anger. "Was it not," he wrote, "for pre-
serving the resemblance of particular persons, painting
would not be known in the place. The people generally regard it no more than any other useful trade,
as they sometimes term it, like that of a carpenter, tailor, or shrew-maker [shoe-maker?], not as one of the
most noble arts in the world. Which is not a little mortifying to me. While the arts are so disregarded, I can
hope for nothing either to encourage or assist me in
my studies but what I receive from a thousand leagues'
distance, and be my improvements what they will, I
shall not be benefited by them in this country, neither in point of fortune nor fame."

It is a lonely task to perfect your art in a country
that already considers your art fine enough, but Copley persevered. Too good a businessman to paint for
his own instruction pictures that he did not sell, he
took advantage of his sitters' artistic ignorance by ex-
perimenting on them. He knew they would accept
the unsuccessful canvases as gladly as the successful
ones, so long as the face was a likeness, "that being
the main part of excellence of a portrait in the opinion of our New England connoisseurs." When he admired a print after a portrait by the Scottish artist
Allan Ramsay, he copied the composition exactly,
and although he required three attempts to make a replica that pleased him, he did not throw away the fail-

ures; into each he interpolated the head of one of his
sitters. Several other of his portraits are adaptations
of British prints.

Actually, the engravings that brought him into
some contact with European art muddled rather than
improved his style. British portrait painters loved to
display the richness and nobility of their sitters; poses
were elegant, gowns expensive, backgrounds cluttered
with the accessories of wealth. Unselfconfident like
most Colonials, Copley imitated the graces that flat-
tered the British upper class, and tried to make his delighted sitters look as much like lords and ladies as he
could. In copying one print after Reynolds, he even included a replica of the little dog Reynolds's sitter
held in her arms, and he put the same number of
pearls in his sitter's hair. These accessories may have
been natural to Reynolds and the lady he painted,
but they were an affectation for Copley and his pa-
troness. Even in pictures he did not entirely imitate
from prints he often cluttered his canvases with imported detail.

In his Colonial embarrassment, he hated to paint
the women of Boston in the clothes they really wore.
He was to complain to Benjamin West that in order
to dress his women in the latest styles he would have
to import the gowns himself from England. But when
for lack of anything better he depicted provincial cos-

tumes, he painted them with meticulous fidelity, for beneath his Colonial feeling of inferiority, beneath the self-doubt that was natural to his character, he was at heart a passionate realist who gloried in depicting things as they were. It is a remarkable tribute to the strength and persuasiveness of Copley's brush that even his adaptations of European prints carry with them the accent of truth. And when in the heat of creation he forgot he was painting crude persons in a crude technique, his portraits reveal great strength and sincerity of personal vision, as his portrait of Epes Sargent shows.

Sargent was a merchant of great wealth. He owned ten of the oceangoing and fishing vessels whose sails enlivened the blue of Boston Harbor. He looked on Sam Adams's rabble with such disdain that when the Revolution got under way, he was one of the Royalists singled out for special persecution. Trying to paint this great man in a manner suited to his position, Copley imagined a columnlike pedestal and told Sargent to lean one elbow on it in a graceful pose. The conception of the picture was thus suitably elegant, but the execution went completely wrong according to aristocratic standards. Instead of leaning like a willow bent by a perfumed breeze, the merchant is shown as a heavy man, whose weight, bearing down on his elbow, will soon force him to change his position. In the hand Sargent holds before his breast, the fingers are suitably spread for a decorative effect, but Copley became so fascinated with the thick fleshiness of the powerful fingers that he painted them exactly as they were. They are almost obscenely full of blood and life. The face, too, communicates more truth than beauty.

From imported engravings, Copley could imitate poses, costumes, and compositions, but he was forced to work out for himself, by the laborious process of trial and error, those aspects of technique most valuable in achieving shape and the impression of truth and a painterly effect. His figures, though clumsy and occasionally faulty in drawing, have a solidity not to be found in the work of many of his more brilliant English contemporaries. They look as if they had been hewn with an ax from the hard wood of American forests. What if the silk of his sitters' gowns lacks the soft sheen of silk, but seems rather a hard, solid substance carved by the woodcutter into folds that would remain immovable for centuries? This, too, adds to the strength and inevitability of the impression.

Able to secure few hints on coloring from abroad, for color printing had not been invented and what painted copies of European pictures he could see were usually very inaccurate, Copley was forced to work out his own color harmonies. Many of his paintings are experiments in tones; some miserable failures, some brilliant successes whose originality and skill take one's breath away. Finally he developed a personal way of using color: cool metallic hues; greens and tans and russets and grays laid on smoothly over large surfaces. There is none of the surface shine, none of the brilliant contrasts, none of the dashing brushwork which characterized the British school. Copley's color, evolved by the same anguish from the same mind as his brushwork, his drawing, and his characterization, blended with them to give an impression of great power.

Before he was twenty-five Copley had achieved a mature style. His manner was solid, not flashy; it was slow and profound. According to European standards it was naïve, clumsy even, yet it was as strong and straight as those wilderness trees which the king's agents marked for use as ship's masts.

There on canvas are the diverse citizens of the New World, man and woman not corseted to any pattern, but allowed to expand to their true stature. Mr. and Mrs. Benjamin Pickman were a young couple of wealth and fashion, the kind of patricians who should, according to the imported conventions that Copley knew, have been shown standing aloof and noble and cold before a tasteful background removed from the ordinary world by the generalizing alchemy of the painter's brush. Mrs. Pickman, it is true, is given a backdrop of masonry to stand before, but she does not belong there any more than we plebeian onlookers do. A very real sun is plotting to freckle her nose, and she is lifting against it, in the most natural of gestures, a blue-green umbrella. The nose itself shows a pug that takes it far from a drawing master's ideal of noses, while the total face is that of a not too attractive matron who will, unless she is careful of her diet, soon be much too fat. Her expression, far from showing nobility and disdain, is that of a comfortable housewife who enjoys a good gossip, even with her own maid. Her pose is so matter-of-fact that it takes no imagination to visualize her stepping out of the frame into the room beside us.

Her husband is a lanky, spiderlike man. The disorder in his dress is perhaps intended to be nonchalant, but it comes through rather as easy informality. Here, admittedly, is a handsome face, but we do not have to look hard to see under the correct features the shrewdness which enabled this Tory, although driven into exile, to come out of the Revolution richer than he went in.

Copley's painting manner had become finished in its very crudeness. His range, it is true, was narrow, but the effects which he attempted he achieved with great skill. Perhaps because his instruction had come

PORTRAIT OF MARY TOPPAN (Mrs. Benjamin Pickman)
1763. Oil on canvas. 50 x 40.
Yale University Art Gallery, bequest of Edith Malvina K. Wetmore.

so largely from engravings, he was inclined to think in terms of black and white. In his portrait of Mrs. Nathaniel Appleton, he not only accepted this limitation but gloried in it. A sharp eye will notice that Mrs. Appleton's sleeve is not black but dark green; that the chair and the table cover are not gray but a muffled red. Yet these low tints are incidental to the pattern set up by the contrast between the white costume and the black shawl. The sharply defined areas of light and shadow heighten the black-and-white effect. The shapes are strong, full, and inevitable. It would be hard to imagine a picture that had a greater impact of reality.

At twenty-five, an age when most painters now are hardly out of art school, the self-taught Copley had already become the greatest painter ever to work in Colonial America, and one of the most interesting artists of his world generation.

ADVICE BY LETTER

COPLEY, who had trusted his own intellect only because he could find no models to copy, was not conscious of his skill; always he felt that, if he could see the work of the old masters he had read about, his own work would be proved worthless. Even contemporary artists who had European experience, men like West and Reynolds must, he believed, paint twice as well as he. When he heard that some of West's English pictures had been imported to Philadelphia, he considered journeying to see them, but despite his passionate desire for self-improvement he did not go. Was this due to the fear of traveling that impeded him all his life, or to the fear that he could find his own art vastly inferior?

Copley's timidity hampered him in every aspect of his life; he was so afraid of his fellow men that he never had a friend. His intimates were always in his family circle, which was now made up of his ailing mother and his much younger half-brother Henry Pelham. For the rest, there was the long succession of sitters who streamed into his studio, but with them he had only formal association. The seeker for perfection struggled so hard at his painting that he did not talk while he worked, and had he talked, who would have understood him? His mind was absorbed in an art everyone considered a menial trade. No one in the whole city, Copley felt, was capable of appreciating what he was trying to do, and he was overcome by a sense of loneliness when his good pictures were not distinguished from his bad, when the pompous Colonial connoisseurs commented only on the likeness.

Perhaps Copley could have escaped his isolation by surrounding himself with young men who wanted to paint, eager young craftsmen whom he could have fired with his own aspirations and ideals. A few such called on him, but were not encouraged; in his entire life he never had a pupil except his half-brother. He may have dreamed of a woman who would love and understand him, but he certainly was very shy with the ladies. When one of his kinsmen married, the contrast with his own loneliness depressed him deeply; only a desire to reach perfection in his art, he wrote, has "given me the resolution to live a bachelor to the age of twenty-eight. However, I don't despair but I shall be married, as I find miracles don't cease."

Certainly his loneliness, his desire for intelligent communication, helped to overcome his fears so far that in 1766 he sent a picture to London for submission to the Society of Artists. However, as soon as he had entrusted his *Boy with Squirrel* to Captain Bruce, he regretted having done so. He wrote to Bruce that he half hoped the sea voyage had so changed the colors that the picture could not be exhibited, and "I may not have the mortification of hearing of its being condemned. I confess I am under some apprehension of its not being so much esteemed as I could wish. I don't say this to induce you to be backward in letting me know how far it is judged to deserve censure, for I can truly say, if I know my own heart, I am less anxious to enjoy than deserve applause."

Captain Bruce was slow in notifying Copley how the picture was received, but the painter heard from other sources that "none but the works of the first masters were ranked with it. . . . This is an encouragement to me, I confess."

Jubilantly, he wrote Benjamin West to say that he was delighted to have the approval of one "from whom America receives the same lustre Italy does from her Titiano [Titian] and divine Raphael." Of course he had never seen a picture by any of the three artists he compared, but how, in his excitement, could he resist citing the great names he had seen in books? He begged West to correspond with him.

Finally a boat brought Copley two letters. The one from Captain Bruce, having repeated Reynolds's praises, added that the English master had criticized the hardness and overminuteness of the drawing, the coldness of the colors. The other letter was from West himself; it too was full of encouragement, though West wrote that the connoisseurs generally had thought the picture too full of lines, "which indeed, as far as I was capable of judging, was somewhat the case, for I very well know that from endeavouring at great correctness in one's outline, it is apt to produce a poverty in the look of one's works. . . . For in nature everything is round . . . which makes it impossible that nature, when seen in a light and shade, can ever appear liny."

Both West and Reynolds urged Copley to come to Europe before his style had hardened into its provincial mold. "You have got to that length in the art," West wrote, "that nothing is wanted to perfect you now but a sight of what has been done by the great masters, and if you would make a visit to Europe for this purpose for three or four years, you would find yourself then in possession of what will be highly valuable. . . . You may depend on my friendship in any way that's in my power to serve."

West was able to advise Copley from his own experience. After he had attracted attention as an infant prodigy in rural Pennsylvania and then as a teen-age professional in Philadelphia, a group of gentlemen

BOY WITH SQUIRREL
1765. Oil on canvas. 30¼ x 25.
Private collection.

had, in their eagerness to further American culture, subscribed to a fund that would enable the exceptional youth to study abroad. Reaching Italy at the age of twenty-two, West absorbed Old World teachings so rapidly that the art critics in Rome were soon calling him "The American Raphael." When he carried with him to London his new style, which expressed American ideas in European techniques, fame rode with him in the coach. By the time Copley sent over his *Boy with Squirrel,* West had solidified his worldly power by establishing a close friendship with England's most powerful patron, with the very king who was to do so much to force the American Revolution, George III. Nor was the world at large stinting with its praises of the transplanted American. In many European nations, connoisseurs considered West the living painter who was most likely to restore to art the glory and dignity of the old masters.

At last in communication with someone he felt would understand, Copley poured out in letters to West complaints about the lack of taste in America and the scarcity of good pictures to study. Then he begged his new friend to explain various points that had puzzled him in books on painting. "I shall be exceeding glad," he wrote, "to know in general what the present state of painting in Italy is; whether the living masters are excellent as the dead have been. It is not possible my curiosity can be satisfied in this by anybody but yourself, not having any correspondence with any whose judgment is sufficient to satisfy me."

Taking to heart all the criticisms West and Reynolds had sent him, Copley determined to obviate them all in the full length of a little girl that he painted for the next London exhibition. Since Reynolds had called his colors cold, he used bright tints he did not feel, and in an attempt to keep the figure from standing out in a manner that could be called "liny," he made the background very conspicuous, confusing the picture with a red-figured Turkey rug, a scarlet curtain, a yellow chair, a spaniel, and a green and yellow parrot. Although this portrait (believed to be of Mary Warner) was one of the least deeply felt he had ever done, he sent it off with a sense of self-satisfaction.

West wrote him that on the whole it had not been as well received as *Boy with Squirrel.* "Your picture is in possession of drawing to a correctness that is very surprising, and of coloring very brilliant, though this brilliancy is somewhat misapplied, as for instance the gown too bright for the flesh." Each part of the canvas, he added, was of equal strength in tint and finish, without due subordination to the principal parts. "These are criticisms I should not make was not your picture very nigh upon a footing with the first artists who now paints." Again he urged Copley to come to

Europe, promising to put him up in his own London house and to give introductions to all the principal Italian connoisseurs. Letters from Captain Bruce notified him of his election to the Society of Artists, and also advised him to come abroad before it was too late.

The prospect of crossing the ocean now stared Copley in the face. He had long mourned the lack of opportunities for self-improvement in America, and now, since his new picture had been considered inferior to *Boy with Squirrel,* he was forced to recognize that he could not profit from criticism by letter. Besides, he was most favorably situated for a European trip: he was a member of the London Society of Artists; the king's painter invited him to stay; he would meet all the most famous Italian connoisseurs.

Yet Copley did not jump at the chance. In his imagination the roads of Europe swarmed with bandits eager to cut his throat. Many years later, he was to write from abroad: "It [is] curious to observe that in all the places that I have [been] in, men seem to be the same set of being, rather disposed to oblige and be civil than otherwise. . . . Robberies are very rarely known to be perpetrated. . . . I do not find those dangers and difficulties . . . so great as people do that sit at home and paint out frightful stories to themselves in their imaginations . . . I find all the difficulty is in setting about such business." But in the 1760's, he had not yet learned this lesson.

Financial terror joined with physical fear to make Copley put behind him his desire to excel in his art for the joy of excelling. Supposing he did study in Europe, he asked in an unaddressed letter that was probably to Captain Bruce, "what shall I do at the end of that time (for prudence bids us to consider the future as well as the present)? Why, I must either return to America and bury all my improvements among people entirely destitute of all just ideas of the arts, and without any addition of reputation to what I have already gained . . . or I should set down in London in a way perhaps less advantageous than what I am in at present, and I cannot think of purchasing fame at so dear a rate."

In another letter to Bruce, Copley harps on the same theme: "I would gladly exchange my situation for the serene climate of Italy, or even that of England, but what would be the advantage of seeking improvement at such an outlay of time and money? I am now in as good business as the poverty of this place will admit. I make as much money as if I were a Raphael or a Correggio, and three hundred guineas a year, my present income, is equal to nine hundred a year in London. With regard to reputation, you are sensible that fame cannot be durable where pictures are confined to sitting rooms, and regarded only for the resemblance they bear to their originals. Were I sure of doing as well in Europe as here, I would not hesitate a moment in my choice, but I might in the experiment waste a thousand pounds and two years of my time, and have to return baffled to America. Then I should have to take my mother with me, who is ailing. She does not, however, seem averse to cross the salt water once more, but my failure would oblige her to recross the sea again. My ambition whispers me to run this risk, and I think the time draws nigh that must determine my future fortune."

Copley wrote West that he was sending him two pictures that would show what improvements he had recently made. The subject of one would be in England; he asked West to compare the sitter to his likeness and decide whether Copley could expect to make his living as a portrait painter in London. "I must beg, however, that you will not suffer your benevolent wishes for my welfare to induce you to think more favourably of my works than they deserve." He had concluded that it would not be worth his while to go abroad unless he would not have to return to America.

When West's reply came, it showed that the court painter was puzzled by Copley's materialistic attitude. The old masters, he wrote, "to a man of powers . . .

are a source of knowledge ever to be prized and sought after. I would therefore, Mr. Copley, advise your making this visit while young and before you determine to settle. I don't apprehend it needs be more than one year, as you won't go in pursuit of that which you are not advanced in, but as a satisfaction to yourself hereafter in knowing to what length the art has been carried. By this you will find yourself in possession of powers you will then feel, that cannot be communicated by words." West added that, in the candid opinion of the connoisseurs, "you have nothing to hazard in coming to this place," but advised Copley not to make up his mind whether he would stay in England until he had finished his studies.

Copley did not answer this letter or send any more pictures to be exhibited in London. A new interest had joined with the discouragement of West's equivocal answer to turn his eyes back to his Colonial homeland. The new interest was love.

GOLDEN YEARS

COLONIAL BOSTON was a British dependency and, like Great Britain, ruled by a few hereditary families who were, however, merchants, not landowners. These families held by royal appointment all the higher offices in the state and looked down on Sam Adams's elective supporters as rabble. Through their English connections, and the complications of the English mercantile laws, they held a virtual monopoly of the trade that was the lifeblood of the Colony. As a poor boy on Long Wharf, Copley had watched the great merchants strut to their warehouses, dressed in imported clothes and radiating the self-confidence of those who are born to command. And if one of them deigned to walk into Mrs. Copley's tobacco shop, how his mother curtsied behind the counter, how the little boy stared with grave-eyed wonder at such magnificence!

But the opportunities offered ability in the rapidly expanding Colony were too various to allow any small group to rule unchallenged. New merchants arose to meet the ever-enlarging demand for goods,

and when they found the path to prosperity closed by
the monopoly the old families held under the English
law, they violated the law, becoming smugglers and
rebels. Rich men like John Hancock joined with Sam
Adams's rabble to form a revolutionary party. Copley,
the poor practitioner of a socially inferior profession,
seems to have sided with these at first; his letters show
that during the Stamp Act riots his sympathy was with
the mob that sacked the houses of the rich.

As time passed, however, the humbly born painter
was taken up by the great. In his eagerness for self-
improvement, he had modeled his manners on those
of his more elegant sitters till no one could tell he
had not been born into the Colonial aristocracy. His
early self-portraits reveal that when he had been
younger, his square face had been too fat, the hair
growing down too low over his forehead. Now, although he had not thinned down into the handsome
man he was to become in middle age, the shapelessness
of his face was giving way to a look of stubborn
power, a bulldog look which successful merchants
must have found more impressive than graceful
beauty. Although his brown-gray eyes gleamed with
intelligence, they did not flit rapidly from object to
object; they fixed in a long, intense stare. Probably
he spoke slowly and with deliberation, the words
heavy with thought.

It was plain that Copley was sober and hardworking, and the number of pictures he was commissioned to paint indicated that he was making a good income. When he called at fine houses to arrange for portraits his sitters got in the habit of asking him to stop in the drawing room. Soon it seemed natural for him to call when he had no portrait to paint. Sitting with his legs comfortably stretched under an imported table, a cup of the best China tea in his hand, he found himself chatting as an equal with gentlemen who had stared through him when he was his mother's errand boy. In such surroundings he forgot his ambition to study in Europe. Benjamin West's advice faded from his mind while he heard wealthy men talk of cargo and the King's Council.

Naturally Copley was impressed by the delicate and accomplished women he now met, so different from the hoydens of the waterfront. One in particular appealed to him. Susannah Clarke, the daughter of a rich Tory merchant, had a gentle smile that made him feel at home in the elegance of her drawing room. She was handsome, but not with the cold, flashing beauty of the great belles; under soft blue-gray eyes her chin receded gently toward a soft white neck. However, she was nobody's fool and this impressed the painter too; her over-large nose jutted out strong with deeply etched nostrils; her brow was high under the upsweep of her fashionably piled hair; and the words she spoke in a harmonious voice were clever. Copley must have known it was foolhardy for the son of a tobacconist to fall in love with the daughter of Richard Clarke. But surely his eyes did not deceive him, surely her lips smiled when he came into the room, surely she listened with interest to his passionate talk of art, to his hungry hopes. When at last he found the courage to propose, she accepted. Probably her father was not enthusiastic about the match, but Copley was able to show that he was a hard workman in a profitable line of business which netted him three hundred guineas a year. On November 16, 1769, he married into one of the leading Tory families of Boston.

Faced with the responsibility of providing an elegant home for his elegant bride, Copley put behind him all thought of going to Europe. Perhaps he was ashamed of this, for when he wanted information about a special kind of oil paint, he wrote not to West, but to an indifferent practitioner who had emigrated from Boston to the Barbados in the West Indies.

His rich marriage helped his business. Soon he had invested some three thousand dollars in a twenty-acre farm with three houses on it, which took in most of what is now Boston's closely built-up Beacon Hill. It was then, according to a contemporary account, "exactly like country, with trees, bushes, shrubs, and flowers." It was a magnificent site, suitable to a prosperous gentleman. His next-door neighbor was John Hancock, one of the community's richest men, whose mansion was a showplace of the city. Copley's front windows looked out on the Common, and his back windows over the water to the hills of Brookline beyond. Many hundreds of acres that are now Back Bay had not been filled in.

A year after his marriage, Copley had a daughter; he seemed tied to Boston and Colonial respectability for the rest of his life. However, the stream of social change was flowing ever more rapidly around him, and sometimes it manifested itself surprisingly in his art. Although Copley was allied by marriage with the Colonial aristocracy, the portrait he painted of Paul Revere revealed — even if the artist did not consciously so intend — an anti-aristocratic attitude which pointed toward the approaching American Revolution.

Paul Revere had not yet had any reason to undertake his famous ride to warn the patriots that redcoats were coming. When Copley painted him, Revere was known as an artisan of many skills: he carved frames, sometimes for Copley's pictures; he published prints, usually based on someone else's designs; and, more grandly, he was an expert and successful silversmith.

It was then the universal practice for men when they sat for a painter to demand that they be depicted, whatever their usual clothes, in the most elegant possible costumes. But Revere and Copley reversed this formula. Although a silversmith had more right to claim to be a gentleman than most artisans, painter and sitter decided that they would emphasize, not suppress, the fact that Revere often labored, in what was then considered an ungentlemanly manner, with his hands. Copley posed the silversmith, boldly dressed for the sittings in his work clothes, behind the table on which he fashioned silver. He was shown holding an example of his handiwork, with the tools of his trade ranged around him. In the art galleries of London a serious portrait conceived in such lower-class terms would have elicited scorn and mirth.

Cleavages between the thinking of the Old World and the New were spreading out across the American scene. In the seaport towns, particularly Boston, mobs were interfering with the English officials who tried to enforce unpopular trade laws that had been enacted three thousand miles away by Parliament. To stop this defiance, the English government sent four regiments of regulars to Boston, where their presence

PORTRAIT OF PAUL REVERE
1768–1770. Oil on canvas. 35 x 28½.
Courtesy of the Museum of Fine Arts, Boston;
gift of Joseph W. Revere, William B. Revere, and Edward H. R. Revere.

stirred mounting bad feeling. Sam Adams published
atrocity stories accusing them of beating babies and
raping young girls. The patriots haled the soldiers
into court on every pretext, while the soldiers hustled
their tormentors around, pricking them with bay-
onets. On March 5, 1770, some small boys snowballed
a sentry on King Street. When he frightened them
away with his bayonet an angry mob gathered. The
sentry called the main guard. Its arrival drew hoots
from the crowd and then a shower of missiles. Losing
their heads, the troops fired, killing five civilians.
The famous Boston Massacre had taken place.

Conscious that an engraving of the massacre would
have a large sale, Copley's pupil and half-brother,
Henry Pelham, designed one immediately and sent a
proof to Paul Revere. When Revere published his
own print of the tragedy, the one that is reproduced
in millions of schoolbooks and is probably the best-
known print ever made in America, Pelham wrote
him the following letter:

Sir,

When I heard that you was cutting a plate of the late
murder, I thought it impossible, as I knew you was not capable of doing it unless you copied it from mine, and as I
thought I had entrusted it in the hands of a person who
had more regard to the dictates of honour and justice

than to take the undue advantage you have done of
the confidence and trust I reposed in you. But I find
I was mistaken, and after being at the great trouble
and expense of making a design, paying for paper,
printing, etc., I find myself in the most ungenerous
manner deprived not only of any proposed advantage,
but even of the expense I have been at, as truly as if
you had plundered me on the highway. If you are insen-
sible at the dishonour you have brought on yourself by this
act, the world will not be so. However, I leave you to re-
flect upon and consider one of the most dishonourable
actions you could well be guilty of.

H. Pelham.

P.S. I send by the bearer the prints I borrowed of you.
My mother desired you would send the hinges and part
of the press that you had from her.

Revere's engraving of the Boston Massacre over-
shadowed Pelham's, of which only rare examples have
come down to the present.

The shooting of unarmed citizens had so enraged
the Boston patriots that militia companies sprang up
and a citizens' army was soon drilling on the Common under Copley's windows. Every evening just as
twilight put a stop to the painter's labors, the air was
riven with the shrill whistle of fifes and the menacing

pound of drums. Round and round, back and forth, the apprentices and dockhands maneuvered clumsily, fowling pieces on their shoulders. The tramp of many feet shook the floor of Copley's living room, and the peaceable artist's heart shrank within him. "I avoid engaging in politics," he wrote to his wife some years later, "as I wish to preserve an undisturbed mind and a tranquillity inconsistent with political disputes." He was not stirred by martial tunes; he hated the idea of slaughter. Looking from the window of his fine mansion at the young men drilling below, he felt again the fear and horror he had known as a small boy when he looked from the window of his mother's shop at the rowdies gouging out each other's eyes on Long Wharf.

It was during these troubled times that he received a letter from John Greenwood, his former rival, who had given up painting and become a successful picture dealer in London. Greenwood said that that city was the artistic center of the world, and that "West goes on painting like a Raphael"; he then commissioned Copley to do a portrait of his aged mother and send it across the ocean to him. He suggested that Copley allow him to exhibit it at the new organization of top-flight artists, the Royal Academy, for which West had secured the king's patronage and which was now overshadowing the Society of

Artists of which Copley had been elected a member.

Thus prodded, Copley's thoughts returned to Europe. After he had completed the picture, he wrote again to West. "I am afraid you will think I have been negligent in suffering two years to pass without exhibiting something, or writing to you to let you know how the art goes on this side of the Atlantic." Having, as usual, complained of the lack of opportunity in America "to prosecute any work of fancy for want of materials," he blamed his marriage and his sick mother for keeping him in so unpropitious a place. "Yet be assured, notwithstanding I have entered into engagements that have retarded my travelling, they shall not finally prevent it."

Confiding to West that Greenwood intended to exhibit the portrait of his mother, Copley expressed dread that the picture would not be well received. The lady was so old that he feared her image would make a bad impression; he would like, he wrote, to show as contrast "a subject in the bloom of youth." However, he could not do so unless he used a picture already in England, a likeness of a young American namesake which had been sent to the famous English radical, John Wilkes. Would people, Copley asked, assume, should he exhibit this picture, that he agreed with Wilkes's politics? "Political contest being neither pleasing to an artist nor advantageous to the art itself,

I would not have it at the exhibition on any account whatever if there is the least reason to suppose it would give offence to any person of either party." West thought it best not to supplement in the exhibition Greenwood's elderly mother with a picture loaned by the radical leader.

While waiting to learn what Benjamin West had decided and how whatever pictures of his that may have been exhibited had fared, Copley made his first long journey; he rode to New York. "The city," he wrote in the words of a true New Englander, "has more grand buildings than Boston, the streets much cleaner and some much broader, but it is not Boston in my opinion yet." He stayed six months, painting about seven hundred pounds' worth of portraits. The most important people flocked to his studio, and even those who had been abroad, he boasted, said his were the best pictures they had ever seen. Copley rose at six, breakfasted at eight, painted until three when he dined, and at six rode out. "I hardly get time to eat my victuals. . . . It takes up much time to finish all the parts of a picture when it is to be well finished, and the gentry of this place distinguish very well, so I must slight nothing." He missed the assistance of Henry Pelham, who usually helped him by painting in backgrounds.

But Copley was making money and that kept him

cheerful. He realized the value of money as only a man who has known poverty can. "You may depend on it," he wrote to his half-brother, "I shall not send my letter in a cover, because the postage will be double if I should." Concerning a lawsuit which Pelham was handling for him, he warned: "Don't be too liberal to the lawyers; they will not do the work one bit the better."

Copley took ten days off to make the pilgrimage he had so long delayed to the works of art in Philadelphia. A copy of Titian's *Venus,* he wrote, "is fine in colouring, I think, beyond any picture I have seen," but, remembering the lesson West had given him, he added: "I must observe, had I performed that picture, I should have been apprehensive the figures in the background were too strong." He was impressed by a *Holy Family* attributed to Correggio. "The flesh is very plump, soft, and animated, and is possessed of a pleasing richness beyond what I have seen. In short, there is such a flowery luxuriance in that picture as I have seen in no other." On his return to Boston, Copley stopped at New Brunswick, New Jersey, where he saw several portraits attributed to Van Dyck.

While he was in New York, West had notified him that his likeness of Greenwood's mother had been well received, and had again urged him to study abroad before it was too late. "I am still of the same opinion that it will every way answer your expectations, and I hope to see you in London in the course of the year."

At last Copley found the courage to write West that he would come; he would take a fishing vessel to Leghorn, study the old masters in Italy, and then proceed to London. West's reply was enthusiastic, but Copley dallied for more than a year until late in 1773 before he could make himself take the decisive step of engaging passage. That the voyage of America's leading painter to Europe was regarded all over the Colonies as a matter of patriotic importance is shown by the letters of introduction to European notables that were sent to him by fellow countrymen he had never met, including John Morgan, Philadelphia's famous physician-art lover.

After years of delay, the Colonial master was poised for flight to Italy, but he did not take off. Instead, he became immersed in a political crisis. His wife's family, the Clarkes, had imported some tea. They were to be guests of honor at the Boston Tea Party.

Was this the true reason for Copley's not sailing? Again and again his family ties had presented him with plausible excuses for postponing his trip abroad, but we may well wonder if these considerations tell the whole story. Fundamental to his entire professional career was a tug of war between the style he had worked out for himself in semi-isolation, and the art of the world centers which he had read about but never seen. The prestige of those dimly imagined pictures was so great Copley was convinced that, once he met them face to face, he would have to surrender his own identity to theirs. In an esthetic sense, he would have to be born again. Surely some part of the mind of this great workman did not wish to abandon everything he was, even in exchange for something better. The creation of the mighty portraits of his American years must have given him satisfaction; he could not have worked so strongly had he not known, in the profound recesses of his nature, that he was working well.

After the failure of Mary Warner had convinced him that he could not imitate foreign art on the basis of the written word, Copley had turned his back on Europe. Although his conscious mind may not have recorded the fact, his pictures show us that deep down he had come to realize that half-measures would not suffice: he must either go abroad or follow his own star. While he dallied in conversation and letter with the first alternative, his painting hand quietly followed the second. For eight long years, he worked with passionate constancy in his homespun manner. These were golden years for his art. By what he called misfortune, he achieved greatness.

Copley's mature American work is characterized by seriousness and intensity. He permits himself no smiles in his paintings, no frivolous passages, even as there are no jokes in his letters. Misunderstanding the gaieties, pretensions, and conceits of the English School, he rendered them with a matter-of-factness that carried them into a different intellectual atmosphere. When, in his full-length of a prominent merchant, Thomas Hancock, he painted a looped red curtain dangling from nothing and in mid-air, he forced himself to believe it. This may have taken some doing, but to do so added immeasurably to the power of the canvas.

As his native realism triumphed, increasingly he banished the fancy conceptions of Europe to the back of his pictures; curtains and urns became dim shapes almost lost in shadow. When about 1760 he had shown Epes Sargent leaning on a column, the incongruous classical symbol had loomed in the foreground. Thomas Amory, executed roughly a decade later, is quite similar in composition, yet the column has become so vague we must look twice to be sure it is there. It no longer bears the sitter's weight: now he leans on the cane he carried every day.

More and more, Copley used light and shadow to focus attention on the parts of a picture he considered important. Amory's face and hands are accentuated with almost brutal strength, while the costume that would have been emphasized by an aristocratic painter is blacked out to a point of artistic danger. Hardly enough body is shown to hold the picture together.

Copley never dared use this approach on ladies. Since the love of females for finery is notorious, he painted their clothes in great detail, but his own concern was clearly less in displaying luxury than in rendering exactly what he saw. Not only did he depict scarf and jewel and silk dress with as much sober intensity as if he were painting them for their own sake rather than as minor areas in a portrait, but he also carried this meticulous, almost scientific attitude to every object he inserted in his pictures. His likeness of Mrs. Ezekiel Goldthwait is supplemented by an exact likeness of an embroidered chair, while the bowl of fruit toward which she stretches her hand is in itself a complete and satisfying picture.

Copley's deep sincerity communicates itself to the viewer and is, perhaps, the psychological basis of his power. As he painted, to an increasing degree, better pictures than he had ever seen, he had been forced more and more to work out his own solutions. Thus he had moved naturally in the directions his own temperament dictated. The result was not the suave and

rounded style of broad culture, but the narrow power of personal prejudice and belief.

Copley revealed an attitude toward the worth of
his fellow men quite different from that which inspired the portrait painters who at the time worked
in more aristocratic countries. They reflected the social organization in which they lived by regarding
personal peculiarities as less important than the class
to which a sitter belonged. To paint a ruler as a chin-
less weakling would be idiotic, since, in fact, he was
the most powerful man in the state. Thus portraitists
subordinated, as of secondary importance, individual
character and peculiarities of appearance. They dwelt
on symbols of rank. The little girl in the fable of the
king's clothes, who startled the bowing courtiers by
pointing out that the king was nude, was not only a
dangerous revolutionary but a fool according to the
conceptions of her time. She should have realized
that even if a king walked naked, he was in essence
beautifully dressed, since elegance of costume was
characteristic of kings.

Copley's world was different. America had no really deep-seated aristocracy, and as the Revolution came
nearer it became ever more characteristic of Americans
to be self-made men who had created their own positions in the world. Those citizens who held power
because of what their parents had done were becoming

so untypical that most of them were, in the coming conflict, to be swept aside. In Copley's world, character and ability were what really mattered. Thus it made sense to depict as realistically and truthfully as possible the personal strengths and weaknesses of the men and women who sat before him.

Although Copley complained of his fellow citizens because they judged a portrait by its resemblance to the sitter, in his heart of hearts he shared their attitude. Never did a great painter occupy himself more singlemindedly with the creation of likenesses. Lacking the technical brilliance that would have enabled him to reproduce the surface appearance of nature —a young girl's dewy cheek, the glisten of light in her hair—he was forced to dig for something more psychologically profound. Unable to describe, he had to interpret. For this arduous labor, he found that a likeness of the face was not enough; a likeness of the body must be added. He made as much use of pose as feature.

So great was his concentration on personal character that his pictures, if hung beside the works of his European contemporaries, would often seem caricatures. The silversmith Nathaniel Hurd leans toward us informally in a bright dressing gown. Over the gleaming silk there smiles good-naturedly the face of a fat man, shrewd, perhaps brutal, certainly intelligent.

Mrs. Paul Richard shows us an old lady who is far from beautiful, but could certainly get the best of a countess by Reynolds when it comes to horse trading.

Copley made visible to our eyes a generation of Americans painted profoundly and truthfully, with neither flattery nor criticism. Living in a period of great social upheaval, he never editorialized; he tried to ignore political conflicts. Yet the curtain that hung between his quiet studio and the battles of the world was suddenly rent from top to bottom. He was forced to play an important part in the negotiations that led up to the Boston Tea Party.

7

THE PAINTER AND THE TEA

Copley's father-in-law, Richard Clarke, was as an agent for the East India Company one of the merchants who had agreed to receive and sell the tea the destruction of which was to be a turning point in American history. As soon as their names were published, the agents became the targets of patriotic fury. "On the morning of the second instant," Clarke's firm wrote to their London correspondent, "about one o'clock we were roused out of our sleep by a violent knocking at the door of our house, and on looking out of the window we saw (for the moon shone very bright) two men in the courtyard." They presented a letter demanding that Clarke and his sons appear at noon the next day at the Liberty Tree "to make a public resignation of your commission. . . . Fail not, at your peril!"

All the bells in the meeting houses started ringing at eleven o'clock the next morning and continued till twelve; the town crier hurried through the streets summoning the people to the Liberty Tree. In the meantime, the group of agents, supported by their male relatives, were huddled in terrified conference in Clarke's warehouse. It is quite possible that Copley was among them. They decided to stay where they were "and to endeavour with the assistance of a few friends to oppose the designs of the mob if they should come to offer us any insult or injury."

At noon the bells stopped ringing; the merchants knew the meeting was assembled, and waited to see how the popular fury would manifest itself. Finally there was a sound of distant shouting that grew louder until suddenly a mob of several hundred men poured into King Street; they gathered in front of the warehouse, and waved a forest of cudgels at the barred windows. After some negotiations, the merchants admitted a committee of nine to the counting room. As spokesman, William Molineaux demanded a promise that the tea be sent back immediately and no duty paid. Despite the roar of menacing voices below, the merchants refused. Then the mob stormed the warehouse. By taking the doors off the hinges, they broke into the lower floor, but "some twenty gentlemen" were able to defend the narrow stair to the counting room. Finally the patriot leaders, who had probably intended only to frighten the merchants, pulled the mob off. Shouting and singing, the brawny apprentices and dock workers disappeared down King Street.

That was only the beginning. When night fell, the Clarke family received another threatening message. A letter of Henry Pelham's thus described the state of Boston: "The various discordant noises with which my ears are continually assailed in the day, passing of carts and a constant throng of people, the shouting of an undisciplined rabble, the ringing of bells, the sounding of horns in the night when it might be expected that an universal silence should reign, and all nature, weary with the toils of day, should be composed to rest, but instead of that nothing but a confused medley of the rattling of carriages, the noises of pope-drums, and the infernal yell of those who are fighting for the possessions of the devil."

On the morning of November 17, 1773, Richard Clarke's family assembled at his house to welcome a brother who had just returned from Europe; Copley was probably present, for it was an important family jubilation. "All at once," a letter to Clarke's London correspondents reveals, "the inmates of the dwelling were startled by a violent beating at the door, accompanied with shouts and the blowing of horns, creating considerable alarm. The ladies were hastily bestowed to places of safety, while the gentlemen secured the avenues from the lower story as well as they were able. The yard and the vicinity were soon filled with people." If Copley was there, he saw the nightmare that had haunted his childhood come true at last; the waterfront mob, the drunken dock workers, the sadistic bullies had gathered to overwhelm him.

"One of the inmates [of the house]," the letter continues, "warned them from an upper story to disperse, but getting no other reply than a shower of stones, he discharged a pistol. Then came a shower of missiles that broke in the lower windows and damaged some of the furniture." A bloody battle seemed at hand, but at that instant some Whig leaders came galloping into the courtyard. They gathered the mob together, addressed them for a moment, and then led them down the street. Deprived of their prey, the rioters shouted over their shoulders threats for the future.

Here was a situation which every nerve in the body of the pacifist painter wished to flee. Having no interest in politics, wishing only to pursue his art in peace, he had remained nonpartisan, friendly with Hancock and Adams though a son-in-law of Clarke. But his long record of taking no sides made him the perfect person to represent the agents in their negotiations with the patriots. When all the merchants who had expected to receive the tea fled to Castle William, the fortress guarded by British troops on an island in the harbor, Copley became their representative in Boston.

He was glad to do so, for he was moved by more than family loyalty. Opposed to violence at the very core of his being, he was horrified by the violent path down which American politics was slipping; he knew that at the end of that path lay civil war. Since it is customary for American historians who wish to glorify the revolution to classify as Tories all those who were not in favor of extreme measures, Copley is sometimes referred to as "the Tory painter." Many writers have explained that his economic interest lay that way, since almost all his sitters were Tories. Actually almost half of his sitters (45 percent) were Whigs. He had friends on both sides. Since his own background was Whig and his wife's was Tory, he saw there was right on both sides. He realized that the English commercial laws were oppressive, but he felt their repeal could be secured by peaceful means. More clearsighted than most, he saw the fallacy in the belief of many peace-loving Colonials that violence can be turned on and off like a tap; that Parliament could be frightened into relaxing its laws and harmony be reestablished.

With the insight of a quiet man who hated all brutality, he perceived that force breeds force. He saw both parties entrenching themselves into stubborn positions that could not be abandoned. He knew that if angry measures were taken to destroy the tea, compromise would no longer be possible. Knowing this, he performed what was for a man of his temperament an act of heroism: he threw himself into the fray and tried, by coming between them, to separate the antagonists.

Tightening his nerves to the point of action, he called on Adams, Hancock and their fellow revolutionary leader, Dr. Joseph Warren. There he argued that a violent solution of the problem of the tea would bring with it a train of calamities whose end could not be foreseen. Did he know that these men understood this well, that they really wanted a war despite the suaveness with which they phrased their desire for ultimate compromise? Probably not. In 1775, after the hostilities had started in earnest, Copley wrote to his wife: "How warmly I expostulated with some of the violent Sons of Liberty against their proceedings they must remember, and with how little judgment, in their opinion, did I then seem to speak."

When talking to the leaders failed, the timid painter forced himself to appear before town meetings. The day after the tea arrived, the patriots assembled in Old South Church to determine on action. Copley argued eloquently for moderation. Yet the meeting voted that the tea must be returned without any duty being paid. This would have ruined the merchants whose ships, according to English law, would have then been subject to confiscation. Copley secured an adjournment to give him time to consult with the agents. These gentlemen, safe behind the battlements of Castle William, were no more eager for compromise than the patriots; they sent Copley back with a flat refusal to make any concessions. His heart heavy, he carried their letter across the channel; he wandered up and down the waterfront in hesitation, past the dark corners that had terrified his childhood. Perhaps that evening he was not conscious where his feet had strayed, for he knew that the lives of thousands of men lay wrapped up in the paper in his pocket. It was Pandora's box; once opened in a full town meeting of Boston patriots, it might loose the calamities of civil war.

For a long time he paced with the slow steps of deliberation, but suddenly his footfalls were rapid in the stillness. He hurried to the landing and took a boat back to Castle William. "Mr. Copley," the Clarkes wrote their London correspondents, "on his return to town, fearing the most dreadful consequences, thought best not to deliver our letter to the Selectmen, but returned to us at night, representing this." He managed to persuade the partners to promise that they would store the tea until they received instructions from London.

After Copley had presented this compromise pro-

posal to the meeting the next morning, the patriot or-
ators expressed great indignation and denounced the
agents, while the crowd cheered and shouted threats.
Copley seemed to be the only silent man in the meeting. Finally he pressed his white lips together, and
rose to ask for the floor. A sudden stillness fell while
all turned to see what the devil's advocate would suggest. If he could prevail on the Clarkes to appear, he
asked, could he be assured that they would be "treat-
ed with civility while in the meeting . . . and their persons be safe till their return to the place from whence
they should come?" The matter was put to a vote,
and the Clarkes' safety assured unanimously. Copley
then moved that he be given two hours. The motion
was passed and the meeting temporarily adjourned.

Copley set out for Castle William with a slightly
lighter heart. Himself a disciple of peace, he was
convinced that if only the adversaries could meet
and talk together, they would see that both sides
were made up of human beings; they would come
to a compromise. It was blowing hard when he
stepped into the boat that was to bear him to the
castle, but this man who feared the sea was probably
too full of the importance of his mission to be
afraid. Perhaps if he could muster his arguments
well enough, he could prevent civil war. The agents,
however, were less idealistic than he; they preferred

to remain behind the fortifications of the castle.

Copley argued for so long that he was very late in returning to the meeting. As he walked dejectedly down the empty street to Old South Church, he could hear the emotional soaring of an orator's voice, followed, as the voice rose in a crescendo, by a roar from the crowd. He knew that his having kept the patriots waiting had not improved their tempers. The timid painter, we may be sure, hesitated for a moment at the door before he took a deep breath and went in.

The orator in the pulpit stopped in the middle of a sentence; there was a mighty rustling as almost a thousand men turned in their seats. Copley's measured steps took him to the front of the hall, but his voice was dry and thin on the first few words he spoke. He said, according to the minutes of the meeting, "that he had been obliged to go to the castle. He hoped that if he had exceeded the time allowed him, they would consider the difficulty of the passage by water at this season as an apology." A dead silence greeted these words; everyone was wondering why Copley had returned alone.

That night Copley described in a letter to his brother-in-law how he had argued, with all the eloquence he could muster, that the agents had refused to appear, not for fear of being attacked, but because they felt that their presence would only further enrage the meeting if they did not do what the meeting wanted. Their opposition to the patriots' demands, he insisted, was not due to "obstinacy and unfriendliness to the community, but rather to the necessity to discharge a trust, a failure in which would ruin their reputations as merchants, and their friends who had put large sums of money in the enterprise. . . . I further observed you had shown no disposition to bring the tea into the town, nor would you; but only must be excused from being the active instruments in sending it back." He had assured the patriots that this promise would enable them to achieve their ends by peaceful means, since if the tea remained unloaded the captains of the ships would eventually have to take it back on their own initiative.

"In short," Copley continued, "I have done every possible thing, and although there was a unanimous vote passed declaring this unsatisfactory, yet it cooled the resentment and they dissolved without doing or saying anything that showed an ill-temper to you." Fifteen days later, however, the patriots dressed themselves as Mohawks and threw the tea into the bay, lighting, despite Copley's best efforts, the fuse that was to detonate the American Revolution.

The only result of Copley's intervention was to make him an object of suspicion to the more rabid pa-

triots. As Henry Pelham complained in his letters, anyone not in favor of violence was branded an enemy
of liberty. During April 1774 the painter entertained
Colonel George Watson, a British judicial representative concerned with enforcing hated laws. Copley
wrote to his brother-in-law that at about midnight,
some hours after Watson had left, "a number of persons came to the house, knocked at the front door,
and awoke Sukey [his wife] and myself. I immediately
opened the window and asked them what they wanted. They asked if Mr. Watson was in the house. I
told them he was not. They made some scruples of be-
lieving me, and asked if I would give them my word
and honour that he was not in the house. I replied:
'Yes.' They said he had been here, and desired to
know where he was. I told them . . . he was gone,
and I supposed out of town. . . . They then desired to
know how I came to entertain such a rogue and villain."

Copley tried to placate the growing mob by telling them that Watson had been to see Hancock earlier
in the day; in any case, he had left. The rioters seemed
satisfied and went off up the street, but they were
soon back, milling under his window and giving the
"Indian yell." Copley leaned out and said he thought
he had convinced them Watson was not there. "They
said they could take no man's word," the painter's let-

ter continues. "They believed he was here, and if he was they would know it, and my blood would be on my own head if I had deceived them, or if I entertained him or any such villain for the future." After much more talk between the artist at the window and the brawny men below, a chaise with its curtains down came galloping up. Its mysterious occupant called to the leaders, conferred with them for a minute or two, and then the chaise moved off with the crowd following behind in a tight, grumbling mass. The street became quiet again.

Copley was deeply shaken. "What a spirit!" he wrote. "What if Mr. Watson had stayed, as I had pressed him to, to spend the night! I must either have given up a friend to the insult of a mob, or had my house pulled down or perhaps my family murdered."

THE TRAVELED ROAD

IT IS A STRANGE FACT that some three weeks after the
mob had threatened his house and family, Copley set
out for his long-delayed trip to Europe, leaving behind in faction-torn Boston his invalid mother, his
half-brother, his wife and four small children. He
had put off his transatlantic studies for years, waiting
for a suitable time; why did he pick this time that
seems most unsuitable of all? Perhaps he felt that it
was a matter of now or never. He foresaw civil strife,
but his letters home make it clear that he did not expect major trouble to come as soon as it did. Perhaps
he hoped to rush through his studies in Italy and be
in a position to support his wife and children in England by the time the Revolution started.

Since the United States did not then exist, Copley
could not be accused of disloyalty to his native land
if he considered escaping a civil war he thought unnecessary.

However, Copley must have sailed with a heavy
heart. Not only was he leaving his family at a difficult time, but he was embarking to face terrors from

which he had shrunk for years; an ocean voyage, life among strangers, the roads of Europe, which he believed crawled with bandits waiting to cut his throat. So dark were his anticipations that the reality he found seemed almost unbelievably rosy; his letters from England were cheerful in the extreme. He was amazed by the genteelness of the public coaches and the inns. The retiring painter, who had never gone out of his way to be friendly to strangers, was deeply impressed by the courtesy with which he was received in London. "There is a great deal of manly politeness in the English," he wrote. Benjamin West invited him to come to dinner every evening when he was not otherwise engaged, introduced him to Sir Joshua Reynolds, and took him to the Royal Academy, where the Bostonian, used to the prudery at home, was surprised to find that "the students had a naked model from which they were drawing."

Starved so long for good artistic talk, he plunged into endless discussions with his English colleagues. The thirty-six-year-old Colonial, who had already painted immortal pictures, asked questions that a modern art student would hardly deign to answer. He had always wondered, for instance, how you executed an imaginative picture containing several figures. "I find the practice of painting or rather the means by which composition is attained easier than I thought it had been," he wrote to Henry Pelham. Before you touched brush to canvas, you made on paper however many small drawings were needed to work out in general harmony every aspect of the composition. Then, having posed living models in the positions dictated by the drawings, you drew careful studies, "not only figures singly, but often by groups. This, you remember, we have often talked of, and by this a great difficulty is removed that lay on my mind."

For all the courtesy with which he was received, Copley felt timid and strange. He was glad to stay with other Colonials at the New England Coffee House, and one of the most ecstatic passages in his letters describes a dinner at the home of the royal governor of Massachusetts, who had shortly before found Boston too hot to hold him. "There are twelve of us together, all Bostonians, and we had choice salt fish for dinner."

When Copley left for the Continent after six weeks in London, he was delighted to go with George Carter, an English painter who he hoped would protect him in the terrifying mazes of Europe. "Mr. Carter," he wrote to his mother, "[is] well versed in travelling, has the languages, both Italian and French. This makes it very convenient and agreeable. He is a very polite and sensible man who has seen much of the world. It is most probable one house will hold us both at

Rome, and the same coach bring us back to England."

However, Copley leaned too heavily on his new friend, for he did not find France to his liking. Although the scenery was picturesque, "the victuals were so badly dressed that even Frenchmen complained of it. . . . You must know those French wines are not so strong as our cider." The continual complaining of his companion irritated Carter. "Sir," he said to Copley, "we are now more than eight hundred miles from home, through all which way you have not had a single care that I could alleviate. I have taken as much pains as to the mode of conveying you as if you had been my wife, and I cannot help telling you that she, though a delicate little woman, accommodated her feelings to her situation with more temper than you have done."

Carter's diary is full of such irritated references to Copley: "This companion of mine is rather a singular character. He seems happy at taking things at the wrong end, and laboured near a half-hour today to prove that a huckaback towel was softer than a Barcelona silk handkerchief. . . . My agreeable companion suspects he has got a cold upon his lungs. He is now sitting by a fire, the heat of which makes me very faint, a silk handkerchief about his head and a white pocket one about his neck, applying fresh fuel and complaining that the wood of this country don't give half the heat that the wood of America does; and has just finished a long-winded discourse upon the merits of an American wood fire to one of our coal. He has never asked me yet, and we have been up an hour, how I do or how I passed the night; 'tis an engaging creature."

Carter continually teased Copley because he knew no language but English, and the two men quarreled like children about the merits of their respective countries. Sarcastically, Carter describes Copley holding forth on the future of America, insisting that in less than a hundred years it would have an independent government, and that "the woods will be cleared, and lying in the same latitude, they shall have the same air as in the South of France. Art would then be encouraged there and great artists arrive."

Here is Copley's traveling costume as Carter described it: "He had on one of those white French bonnets which, turned on one side, admit of being pulled over the ears; under this was a yellow and red silk handkerchief, with a large Catherine-wheel flambeaued upon it, such as may be seen upon the necks of those delicate ladies who cry Malton oysters — this flowed half-way down his back. He wore a red brown or rather cinnamon greatcoat with a friar's cape, and worsted binding of a yellowish white; it hung near his heels, out of which peeped his boots. Under his arm he carried the sword which he bought in Paris [for protection against bandits, we may be sure], and a hickory stick with an ivory head. Joined to this dress, he was very thin, pale, a little pock-marked, prominent eyebrows, small eyes which after fatigue seemed a day's march in his head."

Copley soon lost his high opinion of his companion. "He was," the Colonial wrote, "a sort of snail which crawled over a man in his sleep, and left its slime and no more."

From Genoa, the last major stop before he reached Rome, Copley poured out his loneliness and ambition to his wife. "I am happy to be so near the end of my journey. Though not fatigued, I am impatient to get to work, and to try if my hand and my head cannot do something like what others have done, by which they have astonished the world and immortalized themselves, and for which they will be admired as long as this earth shall continue." But he was afraid that his art would separate him from his family. "As soon as possible, you shall know what my prospects are in England, and then you will be able to determine whether it is best for you to go there or for me to return to America. It is unpleasant to leave our dear connexions; but if in three or four years [in England] I can make as much as will render the rest of our life easy, and leave something to our family if I should be called away, I believe you would think it best [for me] to spend that time there. Should this be done, be assured I am ready to promise you that I will go back and enjoy that domestic happiness which our little farm is so capable of affording."

But the thought of spending three or four years away from home overwhelmed him with emotion. "Although the connexion of man and wife as man and wife may have an end, yet that of love, which is pure and heavenly, may be perfected. Not that my love is not as perfect as it can be in the present state, but we may be capable of loving more by being more conformed to the infinite source of love. I am very anxious lest you suffer by my absence."

In Rome Copley rushed to the galleries and stared for hours at the paintings of the old masters. All his life he had believed that greatness existed only in Europe and the past. Faced at last with the pictures about whose glories he had read, he felt a determination to revise drastically the technique he had laboriously worked out for himself during long years of isolation; the style that was to do most to make him immortal now seemed of little value. He preferred to imitate famous artists, especially the Carraccis and Raphael. And he adhered to this determination, although like West before him he did not find the old masters as wonderful as he had dreamed they would be. He wrote to Pelham that the difference between Titian and Raphael and the common run of painters was not so great as he had been led to suppose by the fame they enjoyed.

The first picture he painted in Italy, a double portrait of Mr. and Mrs. Ralph Izard, reveals a confused state of mind. The two faces are depicted with much of the hard, strong realism he brought with him from America, but Mrs. Izard's cheeks are a rich and artificial red. The whole picture gleams more brightly than his Boston canvases, yet the color seems not to spring from the subject, but rather to have been applied from the outside. Copley had often defined his sitters' environments by the use of details: an upholstered chair, a pen, a tool. The Izards' environment was Rome, and in his fascination with that fabled city Copley widened the canvas to include the following objects: an antique Greek vase, a classic column, a richly embroidered curtain, some heavily carved furniture in, the latest Italian mode, the statue of Orestes and Electra he had seen in the National Museum, and the Colosseum done in chocolate color. He wanted to get everything in at once.

Copley knew that according to the European artistic ideas of his time, portraiture, because it was basically unimaginative, was regarded as an inferior form of art. The highest form of art was considered to be

MR. AND MRS. RALPH IZARD
1775. Oil on canvas. 69 x 88½.

"history painting": the representation on canvas of scenes out of the past, preferably events from the Bible or from classical antiquity. It was from history painting that West had achieved his great international reputation. Copley was eager to compete in this most exalted arena.

He resolved to paint the Ascension. This rendition of Christ mounting from earth to heaven being his first religious painting, he had in relation to what he was trying to depict no habits to unlearn. He was able to cast off almost completely his American moorings. The result is an amazingly successful picture which has always been underestimated as a work of art because it is so clearly in the manner of Raphael. Copley showed tremendous skill as an imitator; had he wished, he could undoubtedly have been one of the greatest artistic forgers of all time.

A line of figures in attitudes of adoration and surprise are placed before a softly indicated green landscape. Their robes are gems of brilliant color; dark green, red, emerald, blue. The squatness of their bodies ties them to the earth in contrast with the tall Christ who rises high above them in a swirl of yellow cloud. The picture bristles with the many arm gestures so dearly beloved by historical painters, but perhaps because the canvas is small — a little less than three feet by a little over two — they are unobtrusive.

Christ is ascending — you cannot in your imagination pull him down — and the figure doubled up with emotion in the foreground could not be straightened out by a two-ox team.

Copley wrote home that Gavin Hamilton, a leading historical painter from England, had examined the picture. He was "lavish in its praises, and he says he never saw a finer composition in his life, and that he knows no one who can equal it." Copley determined then and there to set up as an historical as well as a portrait painter. He confided to Pelham that Hamilton had told him he was better equipped than West, since he could do portraits as well as history.

Copley was now enamored by the vision of a successful English career. When his wife wrote to him that Boston, occupied by five British regiments, had become highly unpleasant, he replied: "I find you will not regret leaving Boston; I am sorry it has become so disagreeable. I think this will determine me to stay in England. . . . But to give you the trouble of crossing the sea with the children makes me very anxious."

9

ONE COMMON RUIN

Soon Copley had more cause for anxiety; late in September 1774 he read in a London paper that British battleships were bombarding Boston. Although the report was contradicted in the same paper, he was very worried, nor could he set his mind at rest till he received a letter from his wife a month later.

He now arranged to get London papers by every post — once or twice a week — and when they arrived, he picked them up "with trepidation." He wrote to Pelham: "Could anything be more fortunate than the time of my leaving Boston? Poor America. I hope for the best, but I fear the worst. Yet certain I am she will finally emerge from her present calamity and become a mighty empire. And it is a pleasing reflection that I shall stand amongst the first of the artists that shall have led the country to the knowledge and cultivation of the fine arts, happy in the pleasing reflection that they will one day shine with a luster not inferior to what they have done in Greece and Rome." In the same letter he expressed his determination to settle in London. Had he left Boston before he did, he was to explain, "it would have done more violence to myself and dear wife to have fixed in England. But now there is no choice left."

In June 1775 he left for Parma to copy Correggio's *St. Jerome.* No sooner had he arrived than he received a letter written by Greenwood from London saying that civil war had started in America, and that some two hundred people had been killed already. Frantically Copley tried to find some English papers, but none were to be had. All he could learn was rumor, and that became increasingly alarming. "I have seen a letter from Rome," he wrote to his mother, "by which [I] find mention is made of a skirmish having been at Lexington, and that numbers were killed on both sides. I am exceedingly uneasy, not knowing to what you may be exposed in the country that is now become the seat of war. This is the evil I greatly dreaded while I was in America. Sure I am the breach cannot now be healed, and that [the] country will be torn in pieces, first by the quarrel with Great Britain until it is a distinct government, and then with civil discord till time has settled it into some permanent form of government. What that will be no man can tell. Whether it will be free or despotic is beyond the reach of human wisdom to decide."

When a letter came from Pelham, it was not reassuring. "Alas! My dear brother, where shall I find words sufficiently expressive of the distractions and distresses of this once flourishing and happy people . . . My hand trembles when I inform you that [the] sword of civil war is now unsheathed." Pelham, whose sympathies were Tory, then described the battle of Lexington quite differently from the descriptions we find in American textbooks. The British "regulars made a retreat that does honour to the bravest and most disciplined troops that ever Europe bred. The fatigues and conduct of this little army is not to be paralleled in history. They marched that day not less than fifty miles, were constantly under arms — part of them at least — from ten o'clock at night till an hour after sunset the next evening, the whole of the time without any refreshment, attacked by an enemy they could not see, for they skulked behind trees, stone walls, etc., and surrounded by not less than ten thousand men, who most vigorously assaulted them with fresh men. In short, considering the circumstances it was almost a miracle they were not entirely destroyed. When the battle ended, they had not near a charge a man."

Since then Boston, which had remained in the possession of the British, had been besieged and blockaded by the patriots. "It is inconceivable the distress and ruin this unnatural dispute has caused this town and its inhabitants. Almost every shop and store is shut.

No business of any kind going on. You will here wish to know how it is with me. I can only say that I am with the multitudes rendered very unhappy; the little I have collected entirely lost. The clothes upon my back and a few dollars in my pocket are now the only property which I have the least command of. What is due me, I can't get, and I have now a hundred guineas' worth of business begun which will never afford me a hundred farthings."

This news was bad enough, but Copley was terrified lest he hear worse. "It may be," he wrote to his Tory half-brother, "for my fears suggest many terrible things, that you are called to arm yourself. But if you should be, it is my injunction that you do not comply with such a requisition, if this does not come too late, which I pray God it may not . . . I have this exceedingly at heart and trust you will implicitly oblige me in this way. I conjure you to do as I desire! For God's sake, don't think this a trifling thing! My reasons are very important. You must follow my directions, and be neuter [neutral] at all events."

Copley wrote letter after letter to his wife, urging her to leave Boston with the children at once. "I should fly to you, but the distance is too great . . . I find there is a great deal of work in the picture I am copying. My anxiety almost renders me incapable of proceeding with it, but it must be done." Communication was so interrupted that he did not learn his wife had sailed until he received word of her safe arrival in London. "My thoughts are constantly on you and our children," he wrote her. "You tell me you brought three, but do not say which you left behind. I suppose it was the youngest, he being too delicate to bring." Copley had guessed right; it was the youngest, who was soon to die in beleaguered Boston.

When Copley heard that Henry Pelham had stayed behind because their aged mother was afraid to make the arduous trip across the ocean, he wrote him long and eloquent letters pointing out the danger of remaining. The English, he insisted, would "pursue determined methods" because they "so resent the outrage offered to them in the destruction of the tea." If only the patriot leaders had taken his advice! But now it was too late for anyone to retract. Although the Americans would win after many years, "oceans of blood will be shed . . . The different towns will have at different times to encounter all the miseries of war, sword, famine, perhaps pestilence." The only thing to do was to flee while there was yet time.

Pelham's letters confirmed his melancholy prophecies. "Mrs. Copley desired we would write a word when we met with fresh meat. You will form some idea of our present disagreeable situation when I tell you that last Monday I eat at General Howe's table at

Charlestown Camp the only bit of fresh meat I have tasted for very near four months past. And then not with a good conscience, considering the many persons who in sickness are wanting that and most of the conveniency of life."

Two months later he summed up the state of mind of the thousands of peaceful folk whose emotions rarely find their way into history books. "Civil war with all its horrors now blasts every tender connexion, every social tie upon which the happiness of mankind so materially depends. We are now unhappily afloat in one common ruin, and have only left us the mortifying remembrances of those halcyon days of ease and peace which we now in vain wish to re-enjoy."

"We still continue in the same state . . ." he wrote from Boston during January 1776. "Both sides strengthening their works, and preventing the other from receiving supplies. Pork and peas, and little enough of that, still continues to be our diet; a baked rice pudding without butter, milk, or eggs; or a little salt fish without butter, we think luxurious living. Lamenting our most disagreeable situation is the only theme of our discourse. Contriving ways and means to get a pound of butter, a quart of peas, to eat; or three or four rotten boards, the ruins of some old barn, to burn, our only business; and the recollection of having some friends at a distance from this scene of anarchy and confusion almost our only happiness . . .

"I don't think if I had liberty I could find the way to Cambridge, though I am so well acquainted with the road. Not a hillock six feet high but what is entrenched, not a pass where a man could go but what is defended by cannon. Fences pulled down, houses removed, woods grubbed up, fields cut into trenches and moulded into ramparts, are but a part of the changes the country has gone through."

Doggedly Copley finished his copy of the Correggio, and although his heart must have burned to join his exiled wife in London, he continued the journey that was to prepare him to make his living in that sophisticated city. He went to Mantua, Venice, Innsbruck, Augsburg, Stuttgart, Mannheim, Coblenz, Cologne, Düsseldorf, Utrecht, Amsterdam, Leiden, Rotterdam, Antwerp, Brussels, Ghent, Bruges, Lille, and then hurried through Paris to London, arriving late in 1775.

It was a great joy to embrace his wife and children, but the reunited family could find no high spirits with which to face the future in the strange and difficult city to which they had fled. Most of their relations and friends, all the world they had ever known, were menaced and racked by civil war. "As to England," Mrs. Copley wrote to Henry Pelham, "you must not expect from me any account of it at present, for my thoughts are so intent upon America that at times I can scarcely realize myself to be out of it. I have not had the least inclination to visit any of the public places of entertainment . . . for I think we are so made for each other that we cannot be happy when we have reason to think our friends are exposed to distress . . . Every account increases my distress. I pray heaven to prepare me for all events!"

AN OLD DOG AND NEW TRICKS

To CELEBRATE his reunion in London with many members of his family, Copley painted a group portrait. His eldest daughter stands in the foreground, while to the viewer's right the painter's wife is shown being embraced by the two smaller children who had come with her to England. At the left sits his father-in-law holding a baby originally intended to represent the child left behind in Boston. At about the time that Copley learned that this child had died, his wife presented him with a new baby whose likeness he painted into the picture. He shows himself standing in the background behind his father-in-law, holding in his hands some papers symbolic of his profession.

This picture expresses happy domesticity, probably all the more deeply felt by the painter because, when he stepped out of his door, the environment in which he moved was hardly cheering. Like many an American after him, the painter found that the English who had received him so politely when he was a stranger were not eager to make him a friend. Although not a Tory, he was forced to rely on the society of the Tory refugees. He attended the weekly dinners of their "Loyalist Club," where talk ran drearily on war and poverty; the exiles whose American property had been confiscated by the revolutionaries, complained of empty purses with all the ardor of the new poor. Copley was able to join in the chorus, for his savings were tied up in Boston real estate and his painting brought in little money. Although he was elected an associate of the Royal Academy over twenty other candidates, and although Benjamin West used all his vast influence to get him commissions, he made so little that his impoverished father-in-law had to help in his support.

Copley soon found himself in a mood where even slight mishaps seemed overwhelming. To cut short his Roman stay, he had bought plaster casts of the most important antique statues to study in London. They were so badly packed, however, that they arrived in fragments, a misfortune which, his son tells us, "he never ceased to regret during the whole course of his after life."

With increasing intensity Copley mourned the casts that were to smooth out the roughness of his Colonial technique, for his lack of immediate success in England further convinced him that he must abandon the crudely honest approach he had worked out for himself in isolation and learn to paint like fashionable Brit-

THE COPLEY FAMILY

1776–1777. Oil on canvas. 72½ x 90⅜.

National Gallery of Art, Washington, D.C.; Andrew Mellon Fund.

ish artists. This was not easy to achieve. For Copley had been formed by his Colonial environment as surely as a tree is shaped by the soil in which it grows. He could rent a house in the right part of London, he could buy his clothes from a good English tailor, he could even modify his Yankee way of speaking; but in the profounder recesses of his mind a bright American sun burned away the mists that softened the English air. He could not help seeing things the wrong way.

The first major subject picture he painted in London was very strange for its time; perhaps he would not have undertaken it had he realized how strange. He had made the acquaintance of Brook Watson, a man who had spent much time in America. That this able and plausible merchant was considered a spy in the British employ and greatly hated by the American revolutionaries, Copley did not know or care. What concerned him was Watson's wooden leg. Its flesh-and-blood predecessor had been bitten off by a shark in Havana Harbor. Watson's description of this catastrophe appealed strongly to the imagination of the painter who had always feared the sea.

When Watson commissioned him to record the bloodcurdling scene in paint, Copley set about the task with great passion and enthusiasm. First he used his new skills to make a series of drawings on gray paper in black chalk heightened with white. He imagined single figures, then combined them. The final drawing was ruled off into squares and transferred to a small canvas on which he painted a detailed sketch in oil paints. Then, at long last, he enlarged the sketch into the composition that was shown the public. He was to build up all his major English pictures in such a methodical manner.

Brook Watson and the Shark is composed on three levels. In the background we see docks partly hidden by a moored ship; a channel, and a headland with its lighthouse. Dim in the distance, these are surmounted by a misty sky which the sun has turned to yellow. The effect of atmosphere, however, is not carried to the other planes of the picture; not even air separates us from that bloody action. The middle of the canvas is filled with a writhing, horrible shape which separates itself on a second glance into a boat filled far past overflowing with men who gesture in anguish toward the part of the picture nearest to us. There, in the bottom strip, we see a naked man being attacked by a shark.

As Copley painted this nightmare which appealed so profoundly to his own fears, he forgot many of the lessons he had so expensively learned from the old masters. The figures, though in violent action, are painted with the wooden, halting solidity of his American years; the colors — cold yellows and greens and blues — have no superimposed sheen of brightness.

Copley would undoubtedly have been one of the most surprised men in all London if he had been told that the scholars of the future would regard this picture as a landmark in the world evolution of styles. When it was painted in 1778, Doctor Samuel Johnson's dictates still typified correct British taste. From this point of view, *Brook Watson and the Shark* was an uncouth expression of physical emotion, as unsuitable as if the American painter had danced with war whoop and tomahawk in the London streets. Proper eighteenth-century subject pictures avoided the present and reconstructed the past. They were populated with heroes or villains well known to historical or literary memory. They showed the ugliness of vice and glorified virtue, telling moral stories concerned with such conceptions as patriotism, bravery, and love for one's family. To show as Copley did the bloody personal misfortune of an unimportant contemporary in a way that presented no possibility for moralizing or sentiment: this was, within the elevated medium of historical painting, revolution. It pointed toward the pure sensationalism, the interest in excitement and horror for its own sake which was to characterize that broad cultural flow which eventually replaced Dr. Johnson's classicism: the romantic movement. The picture indeed was more than a generation before its

WATSON AND THE SHARK (Brook Watson)
1778 (1773?). Oil on canvas. 71¾ x 90½.
National Gallery of Art, Washington, D.C.; Ferdinand Lammot Belin Fund.

time. It foreshadowed the work of the French romantic painters who were later considered great innovators when they produced similar compositions.

French critics claim that another grisly painting of tragedy at sea, *The Raft of the Medusa* by their compatriot J.L.A.T. Géricault, should be considered the opening gun in world-wide romantic painting. Yet Géricault's picture was created forty-one years after Copley's. The two canvases are so close in conception that some critics believe that Géricault was inspired by one of the many engravings after Copley's picture that circulated through Europe.

Although *Brook Watson and the Shark* was so successful that Copley painted and sold several versions, he abandoned the direction of high romantic painting to turn to a less daring kind of innovation. His next major canvas was a further development of the style which had been pioneered in London a decade before by Benjamin West.

As a fellow American, West was like Copley more interested in the present which meant so much to the New World than in the past which fascinated Europe. He had thus broken with the accepted conceptions of historical painting to bring the so-called "grand style" closer to contemporary reality. In 1771 West had announced that he intended to recreate a scene from the siege of Quebec by the British during the recent French and Indian War in America. He would depict the death of the British General James Wolfe which had occurred, with poetic tragedy, at the very moment when victory was achieved.

It had long been conventional to paint scenes glorifying the death of heroes. But the critics and the most admired artists believed that such scenes, if laid in recent times, could not be art unless the resemblance of modern heroes to the great men of the past was symbolized in the way they were clothed. Moderns should be depicted suffering in classical togas or at least in the generalized drapery which the Italian Renaissance had applied to saints and angels. Thus the announcement of a major painter like West that he intended to paint *The Death of Wolfe* as realistically as he could —that he would clothe his characters in ordinary army uniforms—exploded like a bombshell in the London art world. Both Sir Joshua Reynolds and the king argued with West against such rashness.

West replied, "The event to be commemorated took place on the thirteenth of September, 1759, in a region unknown to the Greek and Romans, and at a period of time when no such nations, nor heroes in their costumes, any longer existed. . . . The same truth that guides the pen of the historian should govern the pencil of the painter. . . . I want to mark the date, the place, and the parties engaged in the event."

The finished canvas was approved by the king, and became one of the most popular pictures ever created in England. It tapped the market for news pictures which was generations later to be exploited by such magazines as *Life*. Even the critics backwatered, finding new sanctions for West's realistic approach in the works of the ancients.

The Death of Wolfe, which featured a half-naked Indian in the foreground, was removed from the humdrum of everyday London by its exotic setting in faraway and still quite savage Canada. But in 1778, a dramatic happening that screamed for the painter's brush took place at home. The elder Pitt, the Earl of Chatham, while addressing the House of Lords suffered a stroke from which he never recovered. Both West and Copley started pictures of this scene that interested every Englishman. "Mr. West," Horace Walpole wrote, "made a small sketch of the death of Lord Chatham, much better expressed and disposed than Copley's. It has none but the principal persons present; Copley's almost the whole of the peerage, of whom seldom so many are there at once, and in Copley's most are mere spectators. But the great merit of West's is the principal figure, which has his crutch and gouty stockings, which express his feelings and account for his death. West would not finish it not to interfere with his friend Copley."

Since Pitt's seizure had just occurred in the presence of many local people and in a building which Londoners passed every day, Copley's picture brought historical painting closer to the here and the now, to local contemporary events, than the so-called "grand style" had previously ventured to go. The viewer would have to be interested not by surprise at the unusual but by recognition of the usual. Copley applied all the literal-mindedness that had been the glory of his American career to painting from life likenesses of a horde of peers. These he gathered together into a vast, melodramatic group portrait of the House of Lords.

Dressed in state robes of ermine and scarlet, more than fifty noblemen are gathered around the prime minister, who has just fallen over backward into the arms of his son. The canvas holds together amazingly well, considering the number of individuals included, but it was impossible to carry a unified emotion through such a horde of faces. The picture seems formal rather than emotional. Yet it is startling in the glow of its color, in its movement, and in the concise sharpness of the myriad portraits. It is polished and finished from ermine to feather, from glossy boot and shoe to glistening buckle and star. The technical brilliance displayed is almost unbelievable when we remember that Copley had been painting in the style only a few years.

The Royal Academy supported itself by charging admission to an exhibition held annually. In 1781 the members looked forward to the crowds which Copley's impressive rendition of so popular a subject would bring to their gates. However, Copley, who had already refused fifteen hundred guineas for the picture and had sold subscriptions for twenty-five hundred large engravings, decided it would be profitable to show *The Death of Chatham* separately as an individual attraction, and himself pocket the fees the public paid for seeing it. Choosing the social season when the city was fullest, he scheduled his exhibition at the same time as the Academy's.

Copley's fellow artists were so infuriated that they forced his landlord to evict him from the showroom he had rented. When he found another, Sir William Chambers, the famous architect, wrote him their sentiments: "No one wishes Mr. Copley greater success, or is more sensible of his merit, than his humble servant, who, if he may be allowed to give his opinion, thinks no place so proper as the Royal Exhibition to promote either the sale of prints or the raffle for the picture, which he understands are Mr. Copley's motives. Or, if that be objected to, he thinks no place so proper as Mr. Copley's own house, where the idea of a raree-show will not be quite so striking as in any other place, and where his own

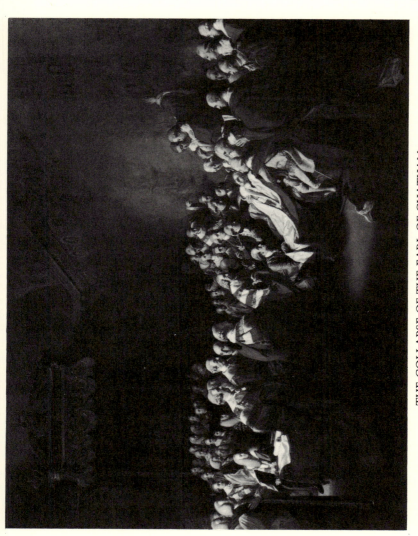

THE COLLAPSE OF THE EARL OF CHATHAM
IN THE HOUSE OF LORDS, 7 JULY 1778
1779–1781. Oil on canvas. 90 x 121.
The Tate Gallery, London.

presence will not fail to be of service to his views."

More than twenty thousand people paid to see Copley's picture, while the receipts of the Royal Academy Exhibition, which contained seven Gainsboroughs and fifteen Reynoldses, fell a third, or more than a thousand pounds, from the previous year. Copley's private show, as the *Morning Post* estimated, made him about five thousand pounds, but it also made him many enemies. When prints of *The Death of Chatham* were completed, it was whispered that they had been distributed fraudulently, the first, sharpest prints taken from the plate not having been assigned, as they were supposed to be, to the early subscribers. All the expert witnesses Copley could bring forth did not entirely silence the rumor.

The merchants, who had worshiped Chatham, flocked to Copley to have their portraits done. He was soon in the full tide of prosperity. He had achieved the greatest ambition of a Colonial by becoming a successful painter in the mother city. Yet he was not happy. Never a man who made human contacts easily, he found the English stiff and hard to get on with; their manners seemed to him overbearing. Used to being the leading painter of a continent, he felt undervalued in a place where others had greater reputations than he. He became particularly jealous of the man who had made his English career possible. Although he frequented West's studio and seemed as friendly as ever, the keen eye of another painter, John Hoppner, observed that whenever West made a suggestion at a meeting of the Royal Academy, Copley opposed it.

As Copley grew increasingly homesick for Boston, the unending denunciations he heard of the American rebels drove him so far from his nonpartisanship in politics that he began to see the revolution he had once opposed as a glorious thing. The former peacemaker became a rabid patriot. When in 1782 he painted a portrait of the American merchant Elkanah Watson, he resolved to place in the background "a ship bearing to America the acknowledgements of our independence." Such a ship should fly the Stars and Stripes, but the cautious painter was afraid to depict that revolutionary flag lest he offend his other sitters. For a long time the picture stood against the wall unfinished. On December 5, however, he accompanied Watson to the House of Lords to hear the king acknowledge American independence. Sitting there with as noncommittal an expression as he could muster, he saw West also in the audience, also holding a vacant look. But when the meeting was over and the king had pronounced, though hesitantly, the fatal words, Copley in great excitement invited Watson to return to his studio. "There," his sitter wrote in his diary, "with a bold hand, a master's touch, and I believe an American heart, he attached to the ship the Stars and Stripes. This, I imagine, was the first American flag hoisted in England."

Although Copley had learned to make his pictures look as if they had been painted with great dash, he was actually still working as painstakingly as he had in America. When the Corporation of London commissioned him to paint *The Repulse of the Floating Batteries at Gibraltar,* an heroic episode that had taken place less than five years before as England fought Spain, he labored on the vast canvas — it was almost twenty-five feet by eighteen — for six long years. A visitor to his studio reported that he was literally fighting the battle there, for he had models of the rock, the fortifications, the attacking ships, the guns, and even of the men. These he soberly grouped into the composition he desired. He stood on a platform, and had fixed his canvas to rollers so that he could bring any part of it within reach of his brush. During 1787 the Corporation of London sent him to Germany, where he painted the portraits of four Hanoverians who had taken part in the defense.

When the picture was finally completed in 1791, he could find no gallery large enough to contain it; he set up a tent in the Green Park. But the crowds who flocked to see the structure angered the fashionable residents of Arlington Street, particularly the Duke of Bolton, and Copley was forced to move to another site. Here, however, his huge pavilion obstructed the view of some householders. Copley was forced to move again. He was in despair, until the king came to his rescue, inviting him to put the tent near Buckingham Palace. "My wife," he is reported to have said, "won't complain." The royal family attended the opening, and during the exhibition some sixty thousand people followed their example. Again Copley offered competition with a Royal Academy show, and took away so much business that it was a failure.

However, such successes did not lead Copley to abandon portraiture. The likenesses he painted now were both more various and more uneven than those he had produced in America. Often he had difficulties with his British sitters. Since in Boston amusements had been few, people had been willing to pose for many long hours. Londoners, however, were beckoned by many diversions. Handling their brushes like fencing foils, English artists amused their sitters by exhibitions of manual dexterity, and finished a face in a few hours. While yet in Boston, Copley had written that his pictures "are almost always good in proportion to the time I give them." But he could no longer walk close to a sitter again and again, soberly matching each color to the face before he put the tint down on canvas. Only rarely was he given an opportunity to think deeply. To compete with his rivals, he had to work with a speed quite foreign to his old New England ways.

Under the circumstances, he did remarkably well. The problems he faced in some of his English portraits and how he dealt with them are exemplified in his likeness of Augustus Brine. The twelve-year-old boy who strutted into his studio was an aristocrat, the son of a high naval officer and himself already a midshipman in the Royal Navy. Copley hated the supercilious youngster at sight — a bad start for a portrait painter; but he did his best to turn out the picture that was expected of him.

He placed the lad's slim figure quite grandiloquently in a romantic grotto by the side of a turbulent sea. Holding back his blue naval coat with a negligent gesture, the boy lays his hand possessively on a cannon. The cocky expression of the face and the grace of the body express the sitter's complete control of his wild environment.

The spectator's reactions as he studies this canvas develop like a serial story. Your first emotion is irritation, although you are not quite sure what annoys you. Closer study, however, makes annoyance give way to admiration. In the right background Cop-

MIDSHIPMAN AUGUSTUS BRINE (1770–1840)
1782. Oil on canvas. 49½ x 39½.
The Metropolitan Museum of Art, bequest of Richard De Wolfe Brixey, 1943.

ley painted a stormy sea under a menacing sky. The waves are indicated almost in shorthand by a series of long wavy brushstrokes, but the colors — yellow, blue, brown, and gray — are mingled expertly to give a strong impression of wild water. A ship is sketched in so lightly that you can hardly see it, yet when you do you feel the emotions of the invisible mariners who are handling its wind-torn sails. The organization of the picture, with its compensating movements of line and form, is sophisticated. The boy's costume is expertly done, varying in its color and texture from yellow-buff trousers of a heavy weave to a filmy white collar.

"I must have misjudged this portrait," you say to yourself. "It is brilliantly painted." But when you step back again to get a general view, your annoyance returns. Suddenly you realize what is wrong; the picture is fundamentally insincere. The romantic grotto and the boy's pose before it are alien to Copley's temperament. The face, although more brightly colored than nature, gives a startling impression not only of aristocratic disdain, but also of the artist's strong feeling of dislike. All the superlative ability with which Fate had endowed the painter could not hide his lack of belief in what he was doing.

Others of Copley's sitters were more sympathetic to him than Midshipman Brine, and of them he made impressive portraits that are convincing as a whole. Faces are, it is true, more generalized and prettified than those he had painted in America. And his abandonment of his old grave and passionate clumsiness had resulted in a diminution of brute force. Yet he had gained a poetic glow, a sophisticated sheen that is gracious, decorative, and charming.

Copley now sometimes undertook those group portraits of families that were conceived of as informal scenes of domestic life and were therefore known as "conversation pieces." The most famous of these, *The Three Princesses,* shows a trio of George III's daughters romping with their pets in a garden.

Before he had known how to compose a complicated picture, Copley had been forced to keep accessories down to a minimum; a merchant would have papers and an inkwell before him; a lady would hold an umbrella or a book. Now his skill at bringing many things together in a single canvas gave a fuller rein to his old love of cataloguing objects for their own sake. The three princesses have a dog apiece, and there are two parrots, and a baby buggy, a parasol, and a tambourine.

This profusion annoyed the English artist Hoppner, who wrote, "Is it, Mr. Copley, because you have heard that fine feathers make fine birds that you have concluded that fine clothes will make fine princesses?

What a delightful disorder! Why, you have plucked up harmony by the roots and planted confusion in its stead! Princesses, parrots, dogs, grapes, flowers, leaves, are each striving for pre-eminence and opposing with hostile forces all attempts of our wearied eyes to find repose." So spoke the fashionable portraitist.

However, the leading English historian of conversation pieces, Sacheverell Sitwell, wrote recently of *The Three Princesses:* "As a picture of children it is pure enchantment." He commented on "the freshness and liveliness of the young princess on the left," adding, "The baby princess in her wide feathered hat is not less pretty. The three spaniels sport and play in the foreground. . . . Is there any more charming painting of children than this? Their health and vitality overflow into this gay and cheerful design, up to the doves and clusters of grapes twined around pillars and across the top of the picture. . . . The picture has every quality that should distinguish its English nationality [!] and is, indeed, one of the masterpieces of the English school."

Partly out of a misguided patriotism which makes them want to see failure result from Copley's move to England, partly because little distinction has been made between the works of his best London years and those of his old age, contemporary Americans tend to undervalue his English pictures. His greatest fame, it is true, rises from his monumental American portraits. However, had these never existed, were his reputation forced to depend entirely on the pictures he created during his English years, he would still play an impressive role in the history of art. Entering the London scene when British art was in the middle of its greatest flowering, he became the most exciting historical painter in England. As a portraitist he rivaled or surpassed all the British artists except a few — Reynolds, Gainsborough, Raeburn — of the very topmost rank.

The old dog had learned new tricks with a skill that showed genius. But it had been a great strain.

COUNT NO MAN HAPPY

FAME AND PROSPERITY did not keep the artist from becoming increasingly homesick, and when his two youngest children, who had been born in England, died within two weeks of each other during an epidemic of "putrid sore throat," probably diphtheria, his wife received a shock from which she never recovered. From that time on, she like her husband walked about their elegant house with a perpetually melancholy face. Wild and meaningless apprehensions scudded through the minds of the nervous pair. Although money was pouring in, the specter of poverty haunted them continually; Copley felt so alien to his English environment that he was sure it would rise up and overwhelm him in the end. Eager to capitalize on the American savings he had invested in his eleven acres of Beacon Hill, he placed them on the market and in 1795 was delighted to receive an offer of three thousand guineas, about five times what he had paid. Only after he had accepted the offer and a thousand-dollar deposit did he learn that the new State House was to be built on Beacon Hill. What he had regarded as farmland would soon become a flourishing part of the city.

Indignantly insisting that he had been defrauded, he sent his young barrister son, John Singleton, Jr., to America to see if he could break the contract. Now that his last tie to America seemed about to be taken from him, Copley felt a wild urge to return to his homeland, to the land where he would again be the most famous of painters, to the land whose social liberty he had grown so passionately to desire. Although his wife dreaded leaving the mild British climate and the greater comfort of their London home, Copley instructed his son to look into the possibility of their returning to America. He gave the boy a letter of introduction to his old opponent, the extreme radical Samuel Adams, who was now governor of Massachusetts. Adams must have read with amazement the sentiments of the man who had tried to stop the Revolution, for the painter complimented him on having "borne so distinguished a part in promoting the happiness and the true dignity of his country."

After the younger Copley had stayed for a while in Boston, he wrote to his sisters: "Shall I whisper a word in your ear? The better people are all aristocrats." He believed that his father was now too radical "to live among them." And twenty years before Copley had been regarded by many as a Tory!

Although the young man was to make a great career in England in the law, he was unable to reclaim the farm, and its loss seemed so overwhelming to Copley that he gave up all hope of returning to America. Innumerable witnesses state that the transaction in which he got only five times his original investment remained ever in his mind, embittering the rest of his life. Sixteen years later the painter Joseph Farington wrote in his diary that Copley complained that the property he had sold for a few thousand pounds was now worth a hundred thousand. "Upon this he ruminates, and with other reflections founded on disappointments, passes these latter days unhappily."

Indeed, from the time of the loss of his farm Copley's star fell rapidly. In 1798 the war with France joined with the Irish rebellion to suck England into an economic depression that deepened all through the Napoleonic period. Only the most fashionable painters were able to make a living, and even their incomes were greatly reduced. Out of pity, the prime minister excluded artists from the war tax. Copley was not one of the most fashionable painters. After a lifetime of dreading such an eventuality, he found himself on the brink of poverty.

And now, when more than ever Copley needed his skill, a strange blight came over his ability to paint. Each succeeding picture turned out less happily. Still trying to duplicate West's triumphant career, he turned to religious subjects — *Hagar and Ishmael, Abraham's Sacrifice, Saul Reproved by Samuel* — but they were not greatly admired. His new historical paintings did not succeed like the old; he was refused permission to show his *Duncan's Victory at Campertown* in the Green Park as he had shown *Gibraltar;* he had to set up his tent in a nobleman's private garden, and hardly anyone paid to see the picture.

Difficulties with engravers threw him increasingly into debt. William Sharp, whom he had commissioned to make a print of *Gibraltar,* dawdled for years without even starting the plate; the subscribers demanded their money back. And when Copley commissioned a small print of *The Death of Chatham* for sale to the masses, the delivered plate was so bad he dared not publish it. He refused to pay the engraver, and the engraver sued. Bartolozzi, who had made the large print of the same subject, appeared for his colleague. "Do you see, sir," Copley's attorney asked Bartolozzi, "in your own [print] the youngest son of Lord Chatham in a naval uniform bending forward with a tear in his eye and a countenance displaying the agony of an affectionate son on beholding a dying father; and do you see in the other an assassin, with a scar upon his cheek, exulting over the body of an old man whom he has murdered? . . . In one, the Archbishop of

York appears in his true colors as a dignified and venerable prelate; in the other, his place is usurped by the drunken parson in Hogarth's *Harlot's Progress*. In one, the Earl of Chatham is supported by his son-in-law, Lord Stanhope, a figure tall, slender, and elegant; does not the other offer to view a short, sturdy porter of a bagnio, lugging home an old lecher who has got mortal drunk?" Bartolozzi denied all this, and was followed on the stand by "an immense number of engravers" who praised the contested print. Copley's attorney then called many painters — West, Beechey, Opie, Cosway, Hoppner — who insisted Copley could not publish the print without hurting his reputation. In his charge to the jury, the judge professed total ignorance of art, and the jury ruled that Copley must pay for the engraving. Thus the artist lost nearly a thousand pounds.

Since he needed to execute some great work to revive his waning fortunes, he enthusiastically agreed to paint one of the largest conversation pieces in history. It was to show a country squire, Sir Edward Knatchbull, with his second wife and ten children. When the squire said that he missed the likeness of his first wife, Copley, in his eagerness to do something startling, suggested hanging her from the sky as one of a group of angels. Convinced that the longer he worked on a picture the better it would be, and at best one of the slowest of painters, he mulled over every figure for months on end, until Knatchbull's youngest child, seeing him around the house so much more often than her father, made a natural mistake and called him "Daddy."

After two years, the dogged painter began to near the end, but at that moment Knatchbull's second wife died. The squire married again and insisted that his third wife be put in the picture in place of the second, while the second, now also an angel, be suspended in the clouds beside the first. Copley was so eager to please that he laboriously rearranged the composition, but just as the picture again neared completion, Knatchbull appeared to say that his new wife was pregnant; a likeness of the baby, as soon as it came, must be inserted. The bewildered painter, who had put so much effort into the canvas, did not dare disagree; again much of the picture was repainted.

Working with all the relentless determination of his nature, Copley hardly allowed himself time to eat and sleep; he could not even spare a moment to write to his elder daughter, congratulating her on the birth of his first grandchild. "Sir Edward Knatchbull's picture has confined us to London," the younger daughter complained during the heat of midsummer. Life was dull while the painter slaved away interminably and no one came to call. Copley lacked time for friends. "There have been balls, masquerades, and fetes without end in honour of the peace, but I have had nothing more to do with them than reading the accounts in the papers."

Copley completed the picture after three years of toil, and sent it to the Royal Academy exhibition of 1803. On the night of the opening he dressed himself in his best clothes and hurried to the gallery, anxious to savor praise and popularity once more. Sure enough, there was a crowd before his picture. Walking more firmly than he had for years, he maneuvered into position to see their faces, but then his own face grew pale. The people before him were not staring in reverence; they were smiling. Suddenly someone laughed, and at once everyone shouted with mirth; they found the two dead wives suspended from the sky irresistibly funny. When Copley tried to slink away, he felt a hand on his shoulder and saw Knatchbull himself, his face red with fury. People were mocking him, he cried; how had Copley dared show the picture without his permission? It must be removed from the show at once. Utterly discouraged, Copley nodded sadly, and the next day the hanging committee were cursing as they tried to fill with smaller pictures the space where the vast canvas had been.

But Copley's troubles with *The Knatchbull Family* were not done. The third wife now demanded that

SKETCH FOR THE KNATCHBULL FAMILY
1800–1802. Oil on canvas. 25½ x 37½.
The Knatchbull Family Collection.

the first two be painted out. Sadly the painter extended the background across the faces and figures of
the angels he had so carefully delineated. The irritated
baronet then refused to pay for the figures that no
longer showed, insisting that Copley's charge of eighteen hundred guineas for the picture was wildly
exorbitant.

When the matter was brought before a legal arbiter, Knatchbull argued that if Copley had painted
the picture with decent celerity, all the changes would
have been unnecessary; the third wife, the new child,
would never have existed at all. He added that he
had been opposed to Copley's depicting his two former wives as angels; he had wanted them shown
merely as portraits hung on the wall behind him.
Each side called expert witnesses. After eleven painters
and engravers, including Beechey and Fuseli, had
sworn that they considered Copley's charge reason-
able, the arbiter decided for Copley, ignoring the tes-
timony of the principal witness for Knatchbull:
Benjamin West.

A bitter story lay behind West's appearance against
his former protégé. As Copley watched enviously,
West had flourished and flourished while Copley
floundered. West even succeeded Reynolds as pres-
ident of the Royal Academy, thus becoming the
acknowledged leader of British art. When he used

his greater influence to secure a commission which Copley had been seeking through his less powerful friends, Copley's dislike for his former benefactor became a ruling passion. He became a leader in the cabal of artists that fought West in the Royal Academy and finally drove him to resigning the presidency. But after a year of trying to get on without the American, the English artists reelected West with acclaim. Copley's machinations only resulted in making him more than ever unpopular with the connoisseurs and his fellow artists.

Sitting dismally in his empty studio, he cast round for some expedient that would bring back the prosperity he had lost. In his earlier years he had created his color schemes, as he had developed the rest of his technique, through laboring hard to express what he saw and felt. Now he undertook experiments with pigments in an attempt not so much to find new colors that would suit his vision but to discover what was called "the Venetian": the secret of the glowing harmonious colors which had beautified the canvases of artists like Titian. In 1802, Copley's son wrote, "My father has discovered the Venetian, the true Venetian, more precious than the philosopher's stone . . . which the artists of three generations have in vain been endeavoring to explore . . . Henceforth, then, you may fairly expect that my father's pictures will transcend the productions of Titian himself." But despite an occasional flareup of his old skill, the run of Copley's canvases continued to grow progressively worse. The drawing became weak, flabby, and pointless, the coloring watery, the compositions empty in the extreme.

Although he had stood up against it for a long time, the pressure of Copley's English environment had been predominantly against the direction of his genius. London was a sophisticated city, and sophistication is a struggle against reality, an attempt to polish, to veneer, to hide the naked crudities of life. In its higher manifestations, it demands the use of imagination to build for man a more beautiful world. In its lower, it runs to corsets and silks and grimaces. Since Copley had been endowed neither by nature nor by his American upbringing to be a purely imaginative painter — only by using facts as a springboard could he throw himself into the air — there was real danger that as he struggled to succeed in London he would sink to the lower reaches of sophistication and become an artificial society artist.

Throughout his entire career, he had worked best when he had worked most realistically. In Boston, books and imported prints and letters from foreign-trained artists had urged him to attempt fancy pictures. But by the time these voices had reached him from across the ocean, they had become dim and thin. And

Colonial connoisseurs who strove to think in European terms were not quite sure what those terms were. Thus the cloak of traditional knowledge which Copley tried to throw about his shoulders was a flimsy garment that tore easily when he moved, revealing the naked muscles of his natural style. As his American painting grew in stature, it became increasingly literal, increasingly matter-of-fact.

Finally Copley met European art face to face. The first result of this rendezvous, his *Ascension,* showed that he possessed a dangerous skill; he was a brilliant imitator. He could have made a career out of repeating slavishly the formulas of the old masters. For a moment he tottered on the edge of the abyss; then he stepped back.

Although he had been baptized by total immersion in European art, he was too hardened a sinner to reform his homely approach overnight. And there were some aspects of his London environment that worked in favor of his genius. Historical painting, as the style had been modified by his fellow American, West, was imaginative only in a restricted sense. Although they might make some changes for effect, artists tried to adhere to basic historical truth. Copley painted his *Death of Chatham* as a collection of shrewd portraits, and in his attempt to depict the siege of Gibraltar built models of the fortifications in his studio. Even that fierce rendition of terror, *Brook Watson and the Shark,* is fundamentally literal-minded. Far from frightening us with imaginative symbols, Copley makes us feel that we are actual spectators of the tragedy as it occurred.

Surveying the art world of London after his arrival from America, Benjamin West had abandoned portrait painting as too social a pursuit. But Copley, who had made his reputation in that mode, persevered. His English sitters presented him with problems much more formidable than any he had faced in America. The Bostonians had, of course, wanted to be shown as finer than they were, but they were not sure how lords and ladies really looked, and wondered how Reynolds would have painted them. Copley was able to take advantage of their hesitation by following his own inspiration.

The Londoners, however, had no doubts about the kind of likeness their social positions demanded. And Copley, no longer the leading painter of his world, was forced in order to secure commissions to make his technique agree with fashions laid down by better-established artists. More dashing execution than he had ever tried in Massachusetts was demanded; brighter color, more glittering surfaces, more graceful forms. The remodeling of his portrait style was a herculean labor, yet he managed to achieve a compromise between the old and the new that was in itself admirable. The bodies under the more subtly painted silk of his best English portraits remained firm, and he was still fascinated by a crudely intellectual face.

However, it was all very wearing. Copley walked perpetually on a tightrope. Beneath his feet ran the thin wire of realism that kept him elevated; to the left was the abyss of purely social painting; to the right the chasm of imaginative imitations of Raphael. As long as he remained physically strong, though he slipped and tottered sometimes, he did not fall into either.

The deterioration of Copley's art was accompanied by a deterioration in his personality. His work plunged in quality when he lost the health and strength necessary to win a psychological battle which had to be fought over again with every picture.

Copley had always been timid and unsocial, but in Boston he had been universally respected, and he had risen to what was heroism for his character in his attempts to stop the Revolution. Although he had never felt safe in London, he had kept his apprehensions under control and functioned as a forceful and effective citizen. Now suddenly all the weaknesses and fears that had scudded through the back corridors of his mind came out of the shadows and overwhelmed him. The change was observed by diarists who scribbled down that he had become mean, cantankerous, envious, quarrelsome, vindictive. Although he lived to be seventy-seven, at sixty he showed the world all the characteristics of a broken and disgruntled old man.

The stinginess that had always been part of his character became a ruling passion. The Academy female model, Farington tells us, usually got a shilling an hour for posing in the nude. "She is very modest in her deportment, notwithstanding her habit of exposure, and was lately married to a shoemaker. She spoke of Copley's behavior to her, who would make her sit a longer time than she could well bear to, and would scarcely pay her half-price. She had resolved not to go to him any more."

He became so crusty that it was news if he was polite to one of his fellow-artists. "Copley," Farington wrote in 1807, "found me in the room alone and accosted me civilly, the first time in several years. He appeared to me to have suffered much in his faculties; his mind seemed to be incapable of comprehending what was going forward." Three years later, Farington noticed on his face a look of imbecility.

In 1811 Morse wrote home: "I visited Mr. Copley a few days since. He is very old and infirm. I think his age is upward of seventy, nearly the age of Mr. West. His powers of mind have almost entirely left him; his late paintings are miserable. It is really a lamentable thing that a man should outlive his faculties."

For almost twenty years Copley struggled through the twilight of old age. Always lacking money, he painted continually in an unceasing effort to produce a great picture, to secure an important commission. Occasionally he had a nervous collapse, but as soon as he was well again he picked up his brushes and returned to his studio. However, all his efforts were in vain, for the tide had set irrevocably against him. When he asked the king to sit again, His Majesty snubbed him before the whole court. "Sit to you for a portrait! What, do you want to make a show of me?" He spent four years on an equestrian portrait of the Prince Regent that, although it is a startling exception to the usual low level of his later work, no one would purchase. When the British Institution paid three thousand guineas for West's *Christ Healing the Sick,* Copley set to work immediately on a vast *Resurrection,* but the British Institution showed no inclination to buy it. "It makes me melancholy," wrote Mrs. Copley, "when I see his rooms so full of pictures that are highly spoken of, and I think with how much perplexity they were produced."

Copley's son had already started on the brilliant career that was to make him lord chancellor of England and finally Lord Lyndhurst. But for the moment his income was small, and he could contribute little to the family support. The painter was continually forced to borrow from his American son-in-law; the little letters in which he asked for one more loan are stiff with hurting pride. But even the loans that were never refused did not serve to keep up his large establishment on George Street. After the failure of Copley's *Resurrection,* the engraver James Heath told Farington that Copley would have to sell everything he owned, including his house, which was already heavily mortgaged. He pointed out that Copley had become very unpopular as an artist. At about this time Mrs. Copley wrote to her daughter: "We are, indeed, revolving what changes we can make, and whether to quit George Street. The difficulty of leaving our present situation is that it would in a great measure oblige your father to give up the pursuit of the arts; and I fear that if he should retire from them in the latter part of his life, he would feel the want of the gratification which the pursuit has accorded him."

The house was saved by a friend who took a second mortgage on it, but though his studio remained to Copley, it was no longer the refuge from the world it had been. As the painter sat before his canvas in an alien city and heard the rumble of the London traffic outside his window, he sometimes stated that the mistake of his life had been to leave America, to seek perfection by imitating the old masters. He scowled at the paintings of his English years that hung unsold in tiers around him, and turned to look instead at some of his American portraits which he had bought back in a vain attempt to evoke the past. He told his wife that these canvases, which he had once scorned as crude, were better than any of the highly polished works of his transatlantic career.

If only he could paint like that now! But he realized it was hopeless. "He sometimes says," his wife reported, "that he is too old to paint." Yet he had to paint, for in his ambitious youth he had never allowed himself time to learn to play. Work alone could distract his mind from his poverty and his frustrated career. What if the picture that grew beneath his hand was vapid and inane? It calmed his nerves to move the hand. In 1815 his wife wrote: "Your father grows feeble in his limbs; he goes very little out of the house, for walking fatigues him; but his health is good and he still pursues his profession with pleasure, and he would be uncomfortable could he not use his brush."

The tragedy had acted itself out long before the curtain fell. Still the doddering actor held the center of the stage, repeating over and over in dull parody the motions that had been the glory of his prime. He continued to paint and complain, to grow weaker and more senile, but he suffered no serious illness until his seventy-eighth year, when he was struck down during dinner by a stroke. Although it paralyzed his left side, he rallied and was able to totter around a little. Even a second stroke did not kill him. His daughter wrote to her sister: "He may continue in his present state a great while, but it is so distressing that without any prospect of recovery it is not to be wished."

The old man sat stuck up in a chair like an inanimate doll, but his eyes still turned in their sockets. When he felt strong enough to talk, he told his family that he would not recover. "He was perfectly resigned and willing to die, and expressed his firm trust in God, through the merits of the Redeemer." At last God took pity. Two hours after a third stroke that left him "perfectly sensible though unable to speak so as to be understood," the long-wished-for release came. On the ninth of September 1815, John Singleton Copley, one of the very greatest painters America has ever produced, escaped at last from the long twilight of his exile.

Suggestions for Further Reading

THE MOST EXHAUSTIVE and up-to-date life of Copley, which includes a complete checklist of his works, is Jules David Prown's *John Singleton Copley* (2 vols., Cambridge, Mass., Harvard University Press, 1966).

An earlier checklist, which remains extremely valuable, is Barbara Neville Parker and Anne Bolling Wheeler's *John Singleton Copley, American Portraits in Oil, Pastel, and Miniature* (Boston, Museum of Fine Arts, 1938).

Those who would enjoy perusing Copley's own correspondence, mostly with his half-brother, should consult *The Letters and Papers of John Singleton Copley and Henry Pelham, 1739-1776* (Boston, Massachusetts Historical Society, 1904). Other Copley letters are published in an abridged and edited form as part of Martha Babcock Amory's *The Domestic and Artistic Life of John Singleton Copley, R.A.* (Boston: Houghton Mifflin, 1882).

Excellent contemporary accounts of Copley will be found in William Dunlap's *History of the Rise and Progress of the Arts of Design in the United States,* originally published in 1834 and now available in paperback, 2 vols. (New York, Dover, 1969); and in Allan Cunningham's *Lives of the Most Eminent British Painters, Sculptors, and Architects,* originally published in 1829-1833.

The author of this book has published extensively on Copley. The volume you hold in your hands is recast from James Thomas Flexner's *John Singleton Copley* (Boston, Houghton Mifflin, 1948) and the section on Copley in Flexner's *America's Old Masters* (New York, Viking, 1939; paperback, New York, Dover, 1967). Copley is further discussed in relation to the artistic movements of his time in Flexner's *American Painting: First Flowers of Our Wilderness* (Boston, Houghton Mifflin, 1947; paperback, New York, Dover, 1969) and *American Painting: The Light of Distant Skies* (New York, Harcourt Brace, 1954; paperback, New York, Dover, 1969).

A Geographical List* of Public Collections Possessing Paintings or Drawings by Copley

UNITED STATES

ARIZONA
Phoenix, Phoenix Art Museum

CALIFORNIA
San Francisco, California Palace of the Legion of Honor
San Marino, Henry E. Huntington Library and Art Gallery
Santa Barbara, Santa Barbara Museum of Art

CONNECTICUT
Hartford, Wadsworth Atheneum
New Haven, Yale University Art Gallery
New London, Lyman Allyn Museum

DELAWARE
Wilmington, Wilmington Society of Fine Arts
Winterthur, Henry Francis du Pont Winterthur Museum

DISTRICT OF COLUMBIA
Washington, Corcoran Gallery of Art
Washington, National Gallery of Art

ILLINOIS
Chicago, Chicago Art Institute
Urbana, Krannert Art Museum, University of Illinois

KANSAS
Wichita, Wichita Art Museum

MAINE
Brunswick, Bowdoin College Museum of Art

*This list has been compiled from the checklists of the artist's work included in Jules David Prown's *John Singleton Copley*. 2 vols. Cambridge, Mass., Harvard University Press, 1966.

MARYLAND
   Baltimore, Baltimore Museum of Art
MASSACHUSETTS
   Amherst, Amherst College
   Andover, Addison Gallery of American Art, Phillips
      Academy
   Boston, Boston Athenaeum
      Massachusetts Historical Society
      Museum of Fine Arts (by far the largest and most
         important collection of Copley's work)
      New England Historic and Genealogical Society
      Public Library
   Cambridge, Harvard College, including Fogg Art Museum
   Concord, Concord Art Association
      Ralph Waldo Emerson House
   Deerfield, Deerfield Academy
      Heritage Foundation
   Northampton, Smith College Museum of Art
   Pittsfield, Berkshire Athenaeum
   Salem, Essex Institute
   Williamstown, Williams College
   Worcester, American Antiquarian Society
      Worcester Art Museum
MICHIGAN
   Detroit, Detroit Institute of Arts
MINNESOTA
   Minneapolis, Minneapolis Institute of Arts
MISSOURI
   St. Louis, City Art Museum
NEBRASKA
   Lincoln, University of Nebraska Art Galleries

NEW HAMPSHIRE
  Manchester, Currier Gallery of Art
NEW JERSEY
  Newark, Newark Museum
  Montclair, Montclair Art Museum
  Princeton, The Art Museum, Princeton University
NEW YORK
  New York City, Brooklyn Museum
    Columbia University
    Metropolitan Museum of Art
    Museum of the City of New York
    Public Library
    Trinity Church
  Rochester, Memorial Art Gallery of the University of
      Rochester
  Utica, Munson-Williams-Proctor Institute
NORTH CAROLINA
  Raleigh, Hall of History
    North Carolina Museum of Art
OHIO
  Cincinnati, Cincinnati Art Museum
  Cleveland, Cleveland Museum of Art
  Toledo, Toledo Museum
  Youngstown, Butler Art Institute
OKLAHOMA
  Tulsa, Philbrook Art Center
    Thomas Gilcrease Institute of American History and Art
PENNSYLVANIA
  Philadelphia, Historical Society of Pennsylvania
  West Chester, Chester County Art Association

RHODE ISLAND
  Providence, Museum of Art, Rhode Island School of Design
TEXAS
  Houston, Museum of Fine Arts
VERMONT
  Shelburne, Shelburne Museum
VIRGINIA
  Richmond, Virginia Museum of Fine Arts
  Williamsburg, College of William and Mary
WISCONSIN
  Milwaukee, Milwaukee Art Center

CANADA

NEW BRUNSWICK
  Fredericton, Beaverbrook Art Gallery
  St. John, New Brunswick Museum of Art
NOVA SCOTIA
  Halifax, University of King's College

ENGLAND AND SCOTLAND

Dundee
  Campertown House and Estate
Edinburgh
  Stewart Society
Greenwich
  National Maritime Museum
London
  British Museum
  Courtauld Institute of Art
  Guildhall Art Gallery
  National Portrait Gallery

Royal Academy
Tate Gallery
Thomas Coram Foundation for Children
Victoria and Albert Museum
Wellington Museum, Apsley House
Oxford
Christ Church

INDEX